MARIA GRETZER

NICK SKELTON

JON DONEY

BRUCE GOODWIN

LINDA ALLEN

JOHN WHITAKER

PIET RAYMAKERS

HENK HULZEBOS

EMMA JANE BROWN

JOAN SCHARFENBERGER

RENÉ TEBBEL

JOS LANSINK

HARVEY SMITH

JOHAN LENSSENS

NIGEL COUPE

KATI HURME

PAMELA CARRUTHERS

DAVID BROOME

CAPT JOHN LEDINGHAM

JOE TURI

HERVÉ GODIGNON

PHLIPPE GUERDAT

HELENA WEINBERG

JAIME AZCARRAGA

ANNE KURSINSKI

LESLIE BURR-LENEHAM

RONNIE MASSERELLA

DEBBIE DOLAN

MARK TODD

MICHAEL BULLMAN

VISIONS

— OF —

SHOW

JUMPING

VISIONS
— OF —
SHOW
JUMPING

ELIZABETH
FURTH

SBL

SPRINGFIELD BOOKS LIMITED

First edition 1993
British Library Cataloguing in Publication Data

Furth, Elizabeth
Visions of Show Jumping
1. Title
798.2
ISBN: 1 85688 038 9

Designed and typeset by Design/Section, Frome
Printed and bound by Colorcraft, Hongkong

DEDICATION

For my family: my mother who has always given me her unconditional love and most powerful support; my father who has introduced me to the realm of horsemanship; and my brother who has influenced my life and inspired my work more than he is aware of

ACKNOWLEDGEMENT

I would like to thank everybody who helped to put this book together. In particular I would like to thank all the riders, course designers and grooms for their cooperation and encouragement. Without them the idea behind this book would never have been realised. Thanks to Italian journalist Lucia Montanarella, without her generous gift of a mini cassette recorder my job would have been impossible; and to Richard Lucas for being such a positive and caring person. My thanks also go out to all the horses, the real stars of show jumping

FRONTISPIECE: A HUGE CROWD EARNESTLY WATCH AMERICA'S KATIE MONAHAN PRUDENT AND NORDIC VENTURE PERFORM IN AACHEN 1989. THE PAIR PLACED SECOND IN THE GRAND PRIX

CONTENTS

PREFACE

In putting this book together, I wanted to encourage the affinity between show jumping fans and the sport of show jumping. I want to offer readers an opportunity to look at all sides of a working partnership. Riders connect with their horses but we don't really get the chance to see what lies behind this closeness. We watch in amazement how an athlete and his master perform, but we don't actually know what sort of relationship riders and their partners share. We only catch a glimpse of those incredible achievements they seem to pull off so effortlessly.

Horses have always been part of my life, and I derived a lot of pleasure from riding and training young horses. The adrenalin that flowed while competing, together with the feeling of achievement filled my life with satisfaction and delight. Unfortunately my back, that had given me some pain in the past, could not stand up to the physical demands of the sport any longer, and finally resulted in my having to give up riding. It was quite a blow! But nonetheless, I took advantage of this sudden transformation and the close of one thing resulted in the beginning of a new challenge. I travelled to far away places, collected experiences and most of all, I discovered a new channel for my life: photography.

Photographs assure that spectacular moments of a competition get captured and immortalized on film. Considering the advanced technology we have nowadays, some people might argue that photographs are too limiting. I still believe that photography remains a unique phenomenon. What other medium gives the viewer the privilege of looking at a picture, sitting back, and letting their imagination take over? It is interactive in a most personal way; the most obvious reaction is to recall particular memories. But photographs also provoke thoughts, and invoke a particular atmosphere. They are used to motivate and help focus on a specific goal. Of course they also illustrate as well as prove a point. Photographs can also help determine the outcome of an uncertain situation. You might interpret my views as being rather romantic, then again I am a photographer!

To accompany the photographs there are contributions from four of the world's best course designers, the riders featured in this book, and their hardworking grooms. Course designing is a very creative and demanding job that has never really been given enough exposure. I met four very different personalities and found it fascinating to discover that although they express themselves very individually through their work, they share many of the same philosophies. By showing the riders — on some occasions the owners — the photographs, I asked them to share their thoughts, their reflections on the horses, or the locations. I hoped that the riders would disclose some of their inner feelings about their partners and their sport to the benefit of us all. In talking with the grooms it soon became apparent that they, like me, do it for love.

Despite being able to meet all the great characters of show jumping, a photographer's life has its frustrations. We are regularly denied certain positions we have set our heart on working from, and find ourselves restricted to areas where we don't really want to be. They are often positions that I would not have chosen for artistic reasons, perhaps the light isn't as favourable or the angle not as advantageous. We are often herded like sheep during prize-giving ceremonies, but sometimes one simply has to accept the fact and try to make the best of it. These restrictions can mean that ten or more photographers will conglomerate around the same spot and just get the same pictures. I always try to look for the shots that capture the moment and yet are different. It is a challenge to keep a fresh approach to it all.

Other obstacles such as closing off certain areas like the stables — mainly for security reasons — or the competitor's enclosure are recent developments. It makes getting at the right people more difficult than ever. Timing is crucial. Especially when you are dealing with people who are under pressure.

Pressure to me means having to quickly change lenses, films, cameras, check the lightmeter, keep an eye on the equipment, catch the riders I'm after, all in the span of a split second! So it is difficult to do all this, and get the best pictures at any given moment!

When it does all come together it is rewarding, and thanks to being in the right place at the right time I got the chance to talk to all the people involved in the sport and put together this book. I hope that it gives you the feeling that you were actually there too.

Elizabeth Furth

FOREWORD

I have read many equestrian books and looked at many equestrian pictures over the years and *Visions of Show Jumping* is a tremendous book for me, being *Chef d'Equipe* for the British team for the past 23 years. I have relived many moments that made show jumping history: the trials, the tribulations, the heartaches, the sad times as well as the joyful. It is all reflected in the riders' faces and in their quotes, in the grooms and their feelings about the horses. So naturally, to me this book is really superb and I know that it will make good reading and bring pleasure to many many people interested in the equestrian world.

After all those years working with the British team I must say that I still find the sport just as exciting. When I look back on the wonderful riders I have known and the problems of picking teams from the days of Harvey Smith, David Broome, Malcolm Pyrah, Liz Edgar, Marion Mould and I could name many more. Today we have marvellous riders in the likes of Nick Skelton, the Whitaker Brothers and all the good up and coming riders, picking a team is just as difficult. I am probably the loneliest man of the team the night before the competition when I am selecting for the following day's Nations Cup. However, I feel lucky because the riders I have the privilege of knowing, realise the problems that a *Chef* has, and the terribly difficult decisions he has to make. In many ways the riders are quite sympathetic, although some of them are ruthless and feel that they should never be dropped. I pick the team that I feel will do the best and will get the best result for Great Britain. Many times I have been right, many times I have been wrong. I don't expect riders to love me, all I want is their respect; I believe that over the years I have earned that respect.

Nothing is won though if you don't have a good team spirit. Going back to when I first took over as a *Chef* and I took a team out, I remember that they used to jump as individuals. There was no spirit in the team at all. I always felt that if I could improve the team spirit, it would really help our performance. It did. As the team spirit developed tremendously over the next five years it wasn't long before the French and German teams followed suit; it feels good to know that other teams have copied what I have done. I must admit that it made it tougher for

us to win, but it is a sport and we all love to win! I get asked how I feel when I lose, well I can tell you now I feel terrible. I am a bad loser — not outwardly — you will always see me congratulating the winning team, but deep down it hurts.

Everybody laughs at me because I always go to church on the morning of the Nations Cup. I remember the words of Bert de Nemethy, the great American *Chef*: 'I hear you go to church the morning of the Nations Cup,' he asked me whether I prayed for victory and I replied: 'No, I always pray that my opposition take being defeated well!' That day we won the World Championship in Aachen in 1978! Bert de Nemethy had to laugh. I really don't pray for victory. I pray for the riders to go well, and to come out without getting hurt. My main concern is that horses and riders come out feeling fit and well.

I believe that when you read *Visions of Show Jumping* and you look at the wonderful pictures, you will also remember that there are many people behind the scenes: the owners, the sponsors and above all the grooms. They also deserve medals at the end of the day. They all get involved and emotional about winning and loosing. This book shows that feelings are a dominating factor in the sport of show jumping, they are the link between a horse and his rider. It is all very emotional stuff and I am sure that you will enjoy it!

Ronnie Massarella
British Team *Chef d'Equipe*

THE CHAMPS DE MARS SHOW
GROUND, PARIS SEPTEMBER 1991;
THE EIFFEL TOWER STANDS
GRACIOUSLY IN THE BACKGROUND
AS A BACKCLOTH TO THE PARIS
MASTERS. THE SHOW WAS
ORGANISED BY FRENCH OLYMPIC
CHAMPION FROM 1988 PIERRE
DURAND, OLAF PETERSEN WAS
THE COURSE DESIGNER

COURSE DESIGNING

Strangely enough, course designing has become of more interest to me since I started taking photographs, when really I should have been just as interested when I was competing.

The technical complexity of course designing is extremely advanced at top competition level. At home when training young horses, as I mainly did, you build distances that never cause a real problem. When you take novice horses to shows, you shouldn't really encounter any tricky distances up to a certain grade. It starts with schooling the horses by taking them through gymnastic lines. By altering distances and dimensions of the fences, you can teach the horse to lengthen and shorten its stride. You can improve a horse's balance, bascule and leg technique, front end as well as back end. In fact these exercises are tremendously beneficial, not only do the horses improve their technique, riders do too. Riders develop a better seat and a good eye for distances. When training, you do all sorts of exercises to get your horse supple and obedient, for example, you jump out of a figure of eight or a bend line. Gradually you prepare your horse for the technical problems he will encounter in a competition as he improves and reaches a more advanced level.

Ever since I have been photographing top riders, standing in the ring and watching them closely, I have understood the subtle judgement needed to gauge distances. It is worth paying attention to positions and characters of fences, as a certain fence, either by itself or in relation to another fence, will provoke a particular reaction from a horse. Recognising all of this and acting accordingly is what competing is all about: a rider has to know what skill certain distances or certain fences require. Once he has that knowledge, he has to relate it to the different horses he rides. Not an easy or obvious thing at all, because reactions can still vary from horse to horse.

Top competition show jumping really is a form of entertainment. Audiences around the globe want to watch the best partnerships perform. They want to enjoy the occasion. They want to witness excitement. They want to show enthusiasm and support their idols. I believe that most of this can only happen if the courses riders and horses have to perform over, are built accordingly. Not an easy task. Course designers have to study their subject, gathering so much information, experience and knowledge to do a good job. It is a stressful job because a lot of responsibility rests on their shoulders. They can rule or ruin a competition. They can make a class entertaining and enjoyable to watch, or they can just as easily spoil it by designing an unpleasing, rough course. Most course designer are very much aware of their accountability. They respect the horse: they don't want to overface them, but their job involves the generation of questions. This is where the art of course designing comes into play. There is no doubt that some course designers are blessed with a certain feeling for what works and what doesn't.

I find the knowledge and artistry of course designers fascinating. I have a lot of admiration and respect for their craft.

Olaf Peterson

Born in Berlin 1937 into an unhorsey family, other than his mother's unfulfilled childhood dream to ride, Olaf Peterson was encouraged by his mother to enrol in Paul Streck's riding school in Münster at the age of 14. He was introduced to horses under duress and admits that he really hated it at first. But something began to spark and from then on he really grew to love horses and spent every free moment around the stable. The family's modest way of life meant that Olaf decided to work in order to pay for his rides. At the age of 15 he used to go round the houses on his street decoking and refilling coal ovens.

Due to the war, he did not graduate from school until he was 20, and for five years his studies in business management took priority over his interest in horses. After extensive travelling all in support of his career, Olaf entered the family business — they produce stationery — his main objective being to take over. It was only then that he bought his first horse, a five-year old called Amateur. At 27, three weeks before his wedding, he had a bad fall in an 'S' class and broke his vertebra which meant that he was hospitalized for three months, and facing the diagnosis of never riding again. Luckily the outcome of Olaf's fall was milder than first suggested. He did recover.

Amateur was sold to Hans Günter Winkler who quickly sold him on before he ended up in Alwin Schockemöhles yard who wanted a horse for younger brother Paul. The pair won a lot of classes and Paul admits that it was thanks to Amateur that he learned how to ride.

Olaf's credits as a course designer are impressive. He built his first 'S' in 1973; his first international show was Donaueschingen in 1975 and shortly after that he was invited to build abroad, only after building courses for two international shows in his home country. He has built on all five continents. His title of Official International Course Director means that he can hold FEI (Federation Equestre International) seminars. He has also been

OLAF PETERSEN AT THE WORLD
EQUESTRIAN GAMES IN
STOCKHOLM 1990

chosen to be the Technical Delegate at the European Show Jumping Championships in Gijon 1993, as well as at the Olympic Games in Atlanta 1996. He is also an official judge and is on the Jumping Committee of the FEI. His major assignments have been: the Seoul Olympics in 1988, the European Championships in Rotterdam, the 1990 World Championships in Stockholm, the 1985 World Cup Finals of Berlin and then Dortmund 1990. He has built more Volvo World Cup qualifiers and CSIO meetings than any of his colleagues.

He builds 16—20 shows a year, and true to his roots, he 'feels slightly guilty because it means that my business gets neglected. I build courses instead of taking holidays.'

Although course designing has become his second job, Olaf is not a professional course designer. He is an independent spirit and would feel 'too much under pressure' if he was to become a full-time professional. It is important for him 'to keep a certain feeling of freedom' and to be able to follow his line without having to bend to the demands of his employers. Olaf puts his success down to coincidence and to the fact that out of a feeling of jealousy grew this innovative way of building courses, and of putting the best riders to the test rather than seeing who could afford the most expensive horse.

'Show jumping always fascinated me: I kept on buying horses after I knew that I could ride again. From 1971 to 1973 I had two great horses and won some important 'S' classes riding against top German riders in the likes of Soenke Soenksen and Hartwig Steenken. I wasn't the greatest but I won a few classes, and felt pretty comfortable in 'S'. I simply wasn't happy nor really satisfied with the way courses were built. I remember that I really never looked good when riding over Micki Brinkmann's courses. They were so horribly difficult! I am talking about the heights and dimensions of the fences primarily. And if the truth be known, I was never the bravest rider! I must admit that I was even slightly scared when competing in these difficult 'S' classes. So I simply avoided Brinkmann's courses as much as I could and rode elsewhere.

'I also complained a lot. Criticised a lot of the courses that we all had to ride in those days. The first step is that one isn't happy, the second step is that one criticises and the third step is that one starts to think about ways one could change things. When I met Wolfgang Feld who didn't only build cross-country courses then, but also jumping courses and was a pupil of Brinkmann, Feld suggested that I went along with him to assist one day. So I did go along once and I found it great because he also had different ideas, mainly about the line of a course.

'Shortly before a big show in Hannover the course designer fell out and the organizers wanted Feld to come and build. Feld was building elsewhere and told them that he had a friend called Olaf Petersen who had built once and that he was capable of doing it. It was pure chance that I was asked, and built my first 'S' there in 1973. In those days, beginning of the 70s, things were a lot different. One didn't have to pass exams, didn't have to work ones way up the ladder. It was rather a case of OK he can build so send him to build. So I built a few 'S' classes. My courses were new, different and riders were happy. The things one doesn't like jumping oneself, like the famous huge Brinkmann oxers, one doesn't build for others. I simply had a different attitude. For me the main objective wasn't the height but the technicality. I wanted to build technical tracks. I wanted to demand more from the riders and not so much from the horses. I wanted to ask more questions to test the rider's intelligence and not their courage.

'I could never afford to buy an expensive horse. So I must admit that I always looked down with a feeling of jealousy on those who could afford to buy expensive horses and who could therefore jump these huge fences. Out of this feeling of jealousy, I wanted to show those riders that horse power alone wasn't the answer to success in show jumping. I wanted to show those who could afford good horses but who maybe didn't have the riding ability that it doesn't work like that.

Hannover was the turning point, the key experience because I was designing on my own and the riders were happy about my innovations.'

At the time his innovations were unique and soon became Peterson trademarks: 'I didn't build the huge Brinkmann oxers that were filled out with hedges and bushes, I 'de-bushed' them. I built more open fences, maybe even see through fences and I quickly realised that faults occurred by building questionable distances.

OLAF'S STYLE OF INCORPORATING THE HISTORY AND TRADITION OF A SHOW'S LOCATION LED TO THE CREATION OF WINDMILLS ON THIS COURSE AT THE 1987 EUROPEAN CHAMPIONSHIPS IN ROTTERDAM. THE RIDER IS EVELYNE BLATON (BELGIUM) RIDING CONNY

'I incorporated the visual effects. In fact, there are three important components when designing and analysing a course:

The line probably the most important factor: it has to be harmonious, because it is primarily the harmony, the growing together between a human and an animal, that brings the spectators to equestrian sport. Not a straight line down one side of the arena

and then a U turn and back. By designing curves that show harmony and create rhythm, the line can also ask a question of rider and horse. Placing a combination so that the rider has to ride past and jump away from the exit is far more difficult than having to jump a combination that would lead toward the exit that one could build much higher.

Dimensions of course the height and the width

are important. The jumping potential of a horse has to be tested without being exaggerated. I prefer to build lower but more technical.

The visual effects to make it pleasing to the eye. Colours and shapes have an effect on horses. One experiments and notes how horses react to different colours. Poles of contrasting colours like black and white for example are more respected by the horse

than say, pastel colours. A good example was when Bert De Nemethy built this rustic red fence at the Los Angeles Olympics without real contrast, the footing was dark brown too. Things like that cause far more faults. Shapes are important too. A full fence as opposed to an airy fence or fences with or without side wings. I believe that side wings are most important — even when a fence is airy. The horse always needs to orientate itself, and the wings provide this needed guidance. The importance of wings and of decoration was so noticeable at the Olympics in Barcelona; it proved how lost and deprived of confidence horses feel when wings and decoration are missing. Especially on the final day, the final combination with these imposing square towers in vibrant colours. All the other fences were bare which provoked faults and then the contrast to the triple combination caused a real visual shock. The horses backed off. Wings have a great effect on the GO of the horse in the positive sense as well as in the negative sense. So there were these huge square wings, plus the dimensions were big, horses couldn't make the back pole, caught themselves on the poles, well you can surely remember the results . . .

'A particular visual effect, not only asks something new of the horse but also tests the rider — does he notice *why* the horse jumps differently here? The rider must think about the fences when walking the course. He hasn't only got to remember the way from fence one to fence 12 — that the combination might be long or short — he has to consider the influence of the size of his horse's stride to make a distance that might not be exactly right. Success depends on the rider perceiving what is needed and translating it into terms that his horse can happily understand, for example an airy fence will demand a careful approach. The more difficult a distance or the more visual a fence is, the greater the technical precision required. The rider has to define the take off point for his horse. The sport really does demand teamwork between horse and rider. There is no reason why a lesser horse shouldn't look good provided he has a good rider on top! My ideology therefore is to put more emphasis on testing the rider's ability than to test the horse's jumping capacity.

'Ironically a course designer produces something which riders don't like doing. He produces faults for a great number of riders. I push them into making mistakes. So it is understandable that deep down I don't make them happy.

'Riders want to participate at as many shows as possible but at the same time they want to keep their horses fresh. This is why moves to a more technical course are well received. I remember that when a Pessoa or a Broome first rode my courses and said "Boy did we enjoy your course" it meant a lot to me.

The riders made me by recommending me to organizers. It all went so fast and I travelled to other countries. The nice thing was that whichever country I travelled to, I had native, on-site assistants who found my philosophy new, and who also understood what I wanted and they proceeded to follow my way like disciples. I see this as a personal success. It is a very nice feeling! Between 1975 and 1988, in 13 years, I have managed to change the sport not *against* the will of the riders but *with* them.

'Beautiful as the sport is, the presentation of it was simply boring! I wanted to make it more visual, and to create a set similar to the Theatre. After all, the sport is called *show* jumping. The sporting achievements remain the same: 1.60m is always going to stay 1.60m. You can compare it to other nice things in life like eating and drinking. One could be drinking the best and the most expensive red wine, but, the exact same wine tastes much better out of a fine crystal glass than drunk out of a mug. One also drinks with the eyes and I believe that the sport is created with the eye.

'In Seoul, I was able to live out my dream. I had no budget restricting me in any way! I had a contract which committed me to design everything starting with the barriers of the collecting ring. Being able to let your imagination run free meant that I was able to show the direction I want show jumping to take. It was similar in Stockholm. There I was given a budget but I am a business man and therefore I could handle it. My intention is to show that every place has its own character. We are in the unique position, maybe together with golf, to create something that people could recognise on television even if there was to be a sound failure during transmission. In our sport we have a great advantage to be able to show so much more.

'I start thinking of the creation, and of the design of my fences two years before big

championships like the World Equestrian Games. I travel through the country, go to museums, read books. It takes time. One has to find a relationship with the culture and the history of the country. The inspiration for the lines doesn't come overnight either. One tests certain lines. It comes by experimenting during the 20 shows a year that I build, and by watching the riders very carefully. Ideas for lines and fences can change through experience, or because of the change in horses. If there were 5 Miltons, I would have to change. But although I build for the top riders, I have to build for an average. I have to observe the riders and the horses very carefully. The lines as well as the questions put in a course might change. I test in Grand Prix and Nations Cups but it all has to be well hidden of course!

'If I was to build the same course using the same material in Aachen and rebuild it in England having the same riders and horses jumping it again, the results would be totally different. A related distance gets influenced by the nature of the footing — rain or sunshine. You cannot measure that. You have to have a feeling for it.

'I want the public to have emotions. I want them to participate, to get excited. I love to see when the audience backs a certain rider or a certain horse, when they jump with him. It is my aim to create excitement and entertainment. When people come to Stockholm I want to offer them a pleasant weekend and to give TV viewers the feeling of watching a thriller. This challenges me, I consider myself a director in the field of show jumping.

'There is another thing, and I share this with my colleagues. In the last decade we course designers have improved the safety factor. This is due to asking more technical questions, due to improving our materials. To think that the Canadians won the Olympic team event of Mexico 1968 with a total score of 102.75 is just incredible. It is unbelievable for me. I think that we have come a long way since 1968 where the public thought that it was normal to see a team win an Olympic gold medal with a score of 102.75. Now the results are far from that, the sport is much safer and the public enjoys the thrills of it to a greater extent.'

JON DONEY IN ACTION AT HIS FAVOURITE SHOW GROUND HICKSTEAD DURING THE RIHS 1992

Jon Doney

Jon Doney's official title is Senior Course builder of the BSJA. He is one of the FEI's course directors, as well as being appointed Official International Course Designer by the FEI. He is an international judge and of course best known as 'the man from Hickstead', a job he has taken over from his mentor Pamela Curruthers after her official retirement at the Derby meeting of 1987. Jon has also designed courses all over the world: the Australian National Championships, the Spruce Meadows Masters, Young Riders European Championships, the show jumping courses for Badminton and more.

In 1949 Jon was born into a very horsey family. They all hunted. In addition to running a business, his father held a race horse trainer's licence, and his mother and sister were both interested in show jumping. Jon, however, has never show jumped: 'I realised at a very early age that I was no good on top of a horse really.' Having decided that he was 'safer on the ground', he started course building at the age of 15.

It all started as a hobby and was never meant to be a career. He is a carpenter by trade and went into his father's business for a while. Very soon he decided that this wasn't really for him and that: 'The challenge of putting courses up, trying to get the right horses and riders to win was rather nice.' His hobby quickly developed into an occupation that was to take over his life, making Jon feel rather fortunate. He is very dedicated to his job and considers nail biting as his only hobby. Well, not quite because he 'tried golf but the hole is too small!'

Pamela Curruthers has influenced Jon throughout. Before taking over at Hickstead, he assisted Pamela at the World and European Championships held at the All England Show

Jumping Ground. Since then Jon has earned himself great respect: 'Riders say to me that they enjoy my courses because they are never sure what I am going to do next! That is fun.

'When designing for novices, we are part of the trainers — it is important to remember that. When you get to the very top level, you've got to set various problems and tests, but the problems must be solvable.

'I am never worried if a rider hurts him or herself, not seriously of course, but I am extremely worried if a horse does because they don't have the option. The rider does. Safety is the most important thing that we course designers have firmly in our minds. We are all horse lovers. We wouldn't be in it if we weren't, because horses are such wonderful animals.

'My style is to have free-flowing, forward courses. This doesn't mean that you won't have some short distances some times, but I'd much rather watch horses jumping boldly and freely. My courses can be big and you will have some tests where horses have to come back, where they have to have balance and control. I like to have one or two fairly testing related distances in a course. The skill is to work out how many testing problems you want, knowing how to test, to get the right result.

'Getting the right amount of clears is a nightmare. Putting up problems, trying to read your horses, trying to make the track fair, trying to get the right winner on the day. Mind you, the more I do, the more nervous I get! I think the more you do the

less you know. When people come and ask me how many clears are there going to be, I'd like to answer: how long is a piece of string? because a lot of it is luck. Even Milton can have an off day.

'I am a planner really. I have got to do everything on paper first. Obviously you have got to be flexible when you get to the show. I don't decide my distances before I get to the show. Quite often I don't have any inspiration! I have to get up, walk about, look at the garden and come back again, think of new ideas. Part of the fun is to think of new ideas. You must be careful, you can get too ambitious by making tracks too difficult, too twisty. You have to be careful not to be remembered for the wrong reasons.

'Every course designer would lie I suppose if they said they didn't want to build the Olympic tracks. Yes I would probably like to build at the Olympics! I am enjoying myself. I have achieved most things. Now, I think I want to judge more. The other thing I want to do is help other course builders along, hold seminars — mainly for upgrading to international level.

'To be a course builder you have to have a feel for horses. I've been around horses all my life. It is very important that you know what a horse is capable of doing. Not only over fences but also how quickly they can turn, how fast horses can go. When you are measuring courses, you have to know where horses can go safely. It's a fine balance between making courses interesting and going over the top.

'You listen to certain riders more than others.

You have to work out if they have a point, or if they're just saying it for the horse they are riding at the moment. If you think that they're right, you have to do something about it. It is very important to listen because we are all in the same sport to make it work. If we are wrong afterwards for not having changed something, we have to admit it.

'A Technical Delegate is only present at Championships. He has overall responsibility for virtually everything. He is over the jury in what concerns the courses. He should pass the course, see if it is technically correct. He has to meet with the course designer and has to approve the course once it is built. It is important that the technical delegate and the course designer get along. Being a technical delegate is a hard job: he has to coordinate everything, stable, vet, the lot!

'Show jumping has improved so much, horses are jumping so well at the top level. But we can't keep on asking horses to jump higher and higher and wider and wider, so with fairly light material and shallow cups, we are asking more technical questions. Nevertheless, I also like to have a few solid fences and maybe a couple of very open, airy fences in my courses. Some course designers try and use tricks with colours. I don't approve of that. One should never trick a horse. It should always be a fair test. I'd rather play with distances. Not so much in combinations, they are difficult enough as they are. You don't need power, power, power all the time. We mustn't forget that we are in the entertainment business. We must make things look good!'

Linda Allen

Native Californian Linda Allen is modest about her achievements, but deep down she knows about the importance of her job and furthermore she consistently gets abundant proof of how good she really is. Like all successful people, she possesses a strong personality and a shrewd ability to constantly re-evaluate a situation.

Born in 1946 Linda made her way into course designing via a successful riding career. She doesn't really come from a very horsey background: 'Her parents were very supportive of the passion she had, 'my mother always loved horses and was an avid spectator, but they shared my passion financially only to the extent that they were able to.' Linda started riding at the age of ten. She rode lots of different kinds of horses from saddle horse to western. But very quickly took to show jumping — 'mainly because it was hard.' She studied pharmacy for five years at university but decided that she wanted to stay with horses on a full time basis, buying inexperienced horses, developing and selling them on. She went into business with a sponsor, travelling to the east coast to compete.

In the summer of 1979 she spent the season jumping in Europe, based at Alvin Schochemöhle's yard. She rode at the Hickstead Derby Meeting and basically enjoyed herself. She rode for the USET on Nations Cup teams at Spruce Meadows, was listed for the Moscow Olympics of 1980 — the ones that were boycotted by most nations. The substitute games were held in Rotterdam in the Autumn of 1980, but Linda had back troubles and ended up in hospital undergoing surgery.

When asked about her major achievements in her riding career, she modestly answers: 'I was just happy to ride at international level. To have been competitive was a big achievement for me.'

She is a winner of numerous Grand Prix Classes on horses that she trained from scratch, winning two big international classes in one year at the Spruce Meadows Masters.

Linda had always been interested in course designing and started by building on an unofficial basis at novice shows. It was a natural progression to take up course designing professionally. She was asked to design all the courses for the 1992 Del Mar Volvo World Cup Final. She has built on all continents apart from Australia 'only because it never fits into my schedule,' 30 weeks a year are spent travelling, between course designing, judging, holding seminars, giving clinics and doing federation work. This doesn't leave much time for hobbies. Even her spare time is spent working, usually on her computer at home — the objective being 'to write a programme for course designing.' One ambition she has is to get together with an architect to build permanent courses.

While still riding she became very interested in how the course designer influenced the development of the sport as well as the training of individual horses and riders. This, combined with Pamela Carruthers' influence, 'I have a lot of admiration for

Pamela, I picked her brains a lot,' makes her one of the world's best-known course designers.

Linda's main concerns are with safety for horses and riders. She wants to use the competition to develop the horses, and still have them go well at

the end of a week's competition — ultimately sending them away from a show better horses than when they came.

'At championship level, competitors have basically proved themselves by coming to the championship. They expect to get their horses tested; they expect to jump big. The main objective is to separate the top riders. In other competitions, to me the most important part is the medium part. You

THE CHRISTMAS SHOW AT OLYMPIA 1992 WHERE LINDA ALLEN WAS INVITED TO BUILD THE MAIN INTERNATIONAL CLASSES SUCH AS THE GRAND PRIX AND THE VOLVO WORLD CUP QUALIFIER

have to ensure that while you are testing you are not putting something in the course that is going to be dangerous or harmful, or detrimental to the progress of the less experienced horses that still make legitimate mistakes. In a three- or four-day show I am

even more careful that if horses make mistakes it doesn't knock their confidence. I am careful not to ask too much of them. You can overdo it very easily even at top level. I am trying to make a course that gets really good jumping but which won't generate bad feelings at the end of the competition, that even the best horses had too much of a question asked. The competition should finish with the horses as pleased with the competition as the riders.

'There is sort of a limited number of things you can do with course building. But there are so many factors to play with that it is almost impossible to duplicate a course. One is creative with the obvious

things: distances, heights, spreads and general material. The most interesting one is how one fence relates to another. I tend to work on finalising my plan, in some cases even doing my plans, as the show progresses. I find it's very easy for me to do course plans when I am at the arena watching the horses and seeing how they are progressing. I can create a course in a third of the time at shows than sitting at home at a desk, looking at a blank piece of paper! I also get my inspiration from seeing the material that the show provides. Before getting to a show, I might have an idea for an interesting treble combination that I would want to put in the big class, then I see the material and I say that would be much better. I am very flexible. Much more than other people. It is an important quality. Outdoor conditions can change, the ground changes so often that you are forced to be flexible! Organisers change classes around and you are given 30 minutes notice . . . so if you don't know how to do that, you are in big trouble!

'I aim to have no one part of the course extremely difficult, the challenge being not jumping a particular jump, but jumping all of the jumps without running out. When I have a disaster it is having too many four faulters and not having enough clear rounds. I like four faults. As a course builder I like it as much as I hated it as a rider. It is terrible for a rider! As a designer it is a wonderful course because it means that the horse jumped very well. The rider might be disappointed but he doesn't have a problem to deal with. I don't like building a fence where the horse has a problem and where he might

PAMELA CARRUTHERS IS BEST KNOWN FOR HAVING DESIGNED THE HICKSTEAD SHOW GROUND INCLUDING THE UNIQUE DERBY COURSE, AS WELL AS THE SHOW GROUND OF SPRUCE MEADOWS IN CALGARY. SHE ALSO MADE HISTORY FOR BEING THE FIRST WOMAN TO BE APPOINTED TECHNICAL DELEGATE. SHE HELD THAT POSITION AT THE 1988 SEOUL OLYMPICS.

'IT HAS BEEN WONDERFUL TO BE INVOLVED WITH HICKSTEAD RIGHT FROM THE START (1960) FOR WHAT HAS BECOME THE BEST SHOW GROUND IN THE WHOLE WORLD. I ALWAYS FELT THAT RESULTS SHOULD NOT BE ACHIEVED BY MEANS OF DIFFICULT DISTANCES, BUT BY THE NATURE OF THE FENCES. IN HICKSTEAD IT IS THE GRADIENT OF THE GROUND THAT HELPS TO GET THE RESULTS'

end up on the floor.

'I am really only happy when I get a good result but I also think that the rides should be beautiful to watch. I don't like it when the winner makes it look hard. It should look very easy, very flowing and smooth. You set a course where the best rider wins by riding fast and forward.

'You can't please every rider. They usually want adjustments to suit their horses better. There is always going to be something in a class that doesn't suit certain horses and you know that. In general I try to be fair. You can't be too influenced by the riders. Sometimes you have got to be adamant. You can end up going crazy making adjustments for everybody! You have to find the balance between being responsive and receptive to the riders, and not having riders push you around.

'We should be balancing course dimensions with carefulness, with technical riding problems but always helping the rider to manage his horses through the year. It is almost as difficult to manage the older horse's career, choosing how and where to show him in order to give him a long life, than to develop a young horse.

'The adrenalin flows when I watch a class I have built! It goes on for hours, days, weeks! Weeks before building the World Cup Final in Del Mar, I worried about what could happen, trying to anticipate everything, then the night before looking at the dimensions, you continuously question yourself. There are always some horrible classes where six of the first horses go clear or you have got 20 horses without a clear . . . It gives you a lot of grey hair. Not good! It makes me eat too much. I do needle point very fast! I only do it at horse shows, when things are going really badly.

'You never really lose the feeling that you don't know very much about it. In this sport you can be here one day and gone the next because it doesn't matter how many good things you have done in the past, one bad one and you're finished. That really keeps you on your toes!'

Paul Weier

Paul Weier is one of the most accomplished and most versatile horseman in the equestrian world. His career ranges from officer in the Swiss army (Colonel in reserve) to rider, farmer, judge, course designer, Technical Delegate and Honourable Steward General. His list of competitive achievements is endless: he has won Swiss national titles and championships in show jumping, dressage and eventing. He rode his first European three-day event championship in 1957. Since then he has show jumped at four consecutive Olympic Games, he has won the Grand Prix of Rome (1966), Lucerne (1970), Aachen (1973), London Olympia (1974), Bratislava (1979) and the Grand Prix of Lisbon a record four times in a row between 1970 and 1973. He won an individual silver medal at the European Championships held in Aachen 1971, and a team silver medal at the 1975 European Championships in Munich.

His course designing engagements are just as impressive. He designs cross-country courses as well as show jumping courses. Paul has built on all five Continents. His major show jumping assignments are two European Junior Championships in the 60s, the Senior European Championships of St Gallen 1987 and La Baule 1991, the Volvo World Cup Finals of Gothenburg in 1986 and 1993 as well as the Pan Arabian Championships in Damascus in 1992. Paul also holds seminars for course designers throughout the world. And as if all of this wasn't enough, he also runs his own riding establishment with its adjacent Inn and farm in the village of Elgg near Zurich.

THE 1992 BARCELONA OLYMPICS WHERE PAUL WEIER WAS ACTING AS CHIEF STEWARD

Paul was born into a tradition of farming on December third 1934. Apart from running the family farm, Paul's father was the buyer of horses for the world famous Freddie Knie Circus and his mother an accomplished dressage rider and trainer. Thanks to his father's connection with the circus, Paul received his first pony at the age of three. He recalls 'being very scared of riding cross-country up until the age of 14 because I had ponies that were damn cheeky with me and I was afraid of falling off.' Despite his fear he still got excited by jumping competitions because this was where all the crowds were. Dressage was still very much in the shadows. I wanted to be part of the action and once I was given better horses and didn't fall off as often, my courage grew.' Paul's confidence even took him as far as winning a racing championship. 'In those days it was said that if a rider didn't have a feeling for speed, he couldn't possibly ride dressage.'

In fact Paul never wanted to 'only hang around horses'. He wanted to follow in his uncle's footsteps and began studying veterinary medicine. In 1957 he was called up for military service, and joined the Cavalry School of the Swiss army. When the riding instructor of the Military School in Bern died, Paul was asked whether he was interested in temporarily taking over the post. He agreed to it and put his studies on the back burner for a year. 'The one year got extended to three and suddenly I was in the army for ten years and had to give up the idea of becoming a vet.' He was in charge of breaking in and schooling young horses: 'We had 750 young horses per year at a time where the Swiss Cavalry owned a total of 2,500 horses. It was actually a super job for a young man.' He was also in charge of the sports section: dressage eventing and show jumping. His interest in course designing also dates back to his army days. In 1957 the Army held their first-ever course builders' course and Paul was 'thrown into it for being the youngest man around.'

'Course designing started out as a hobby for me. I thought that the knowledge of it would help with the schooling of the young horses. Whenever I was abroad, I took pictures of all the fences I saw, now I have a selection of well over 3,000 slides. A friend of mine used to film courses and I watched many films over and over again. This is really how I learned because in those days you couldn't go into an apprenticeship. I then founded a course designers commission in Switzerland and became its president. We took all the national course designers and drew a plan of how we should go about it all. I became more and more involved and started to hold clinics throughout Switzerland and Germany. Between the years of 1965—67, the best assistant rider I had developed a back problem, so he started to design miniature jumps out of painted metal for me. I have a collection of 300 different fences that I take along in a small box when I travel to seminars.

'There was no doubt in my mind that the concept of course designing had to change. In discussions with Micki Brinkmann and Pam Carruthers, I built with Pam in Mexico, Florida and Persia, we all got together and asked ourselves what should happen. I distributed questionnaires to top riders asking them what they wanted, how they wanted to see courses develop, what the most difficult combinations are, how one should incorporate water jumps in conjunction with fences. From that emerged a newer concept. I believe that since 1957 the whole concept of show jumping must have changed eight to nine times at least.

'My aim was to change these huge oxers from the 70s. They measured up to two metres in width. I didn't mind so much because I had horses like Wulf and Fink, they could easily jump them, but we had the thoroughbreds ridden by the Americans, the British and the French. They used to land in the middle of these parallels. Once a horse landed in the middle, it never jumped again. You came to Aachen and people used to say that any oxer under 1.80m wasn't an oxer. We had to jump our first two-metre oxer at the Mexico Olympics. I was determined to change that. Course designing definitely had to become more horse friendly! Horses did not cost as much in the early days, one didn't care about their welfare as much as we do now. In those days horses had to be able to jump massive fences, sometimes even cross-country fences.

'Today the whole thing is more circus like. It sounds a little exaggerated because it has a slight negative ring to it, but it really is circus like in a good sense. We have to build in a short time and produce a good spectacle, only to have to take it all down again to build something totally new again. I find this interesting and exciting. I have always been a great fan of the circus.

'When I build, I want courses that won't break horses, won't push them to their limits. I remember one year I was invited to South Africa to build the fence for the long jump attempt. Being there triggered off the idea that one had to change the way the long jumps and high jumps were built. I had been to Chile for the celebrations of the high jump record there so I had seen the way the fences were built. Horses are definitely capable of jumping 2.50m, 2.60m or even 2.70m, but not by using six-metre poles that weigh 55 Kilos. The high jump record attempt in Johannesburg was a disaster! I filmed it all. When I saw horses that had jumped 2.30m in training never even got over two metres on the day, and their terrified expressions, it really turned me off. I am against high jump and Puissance! It is unfair for a horse to have to jump again and again until he makes a mistake. I don't really want horses to make mistakes.

'First of all I believe that good, experienced course designers should build the small courses for novice horses. It is like in dressage, the judges that judge Grand Prix should be the ones who judge in the small tests too. This gives competitors and horses the right start and sets them up for a good future. Unfortunately the opposite happens, it is always the young and inexperienced who get to work with fragile stock. This often leads to a bad start and horses and riders find it difficult to follow through to the top.

'When I build for the Volvo World Cup Final or a championship, I differentiate between building for the team event and the individual contest, I want the best ridden horse, with the rider that has shown the best reactions to win. To get to that stage one has to build an awful lot. One has to observe the horses. When you're at a show you have to observe from the very first day. I also keep a detailed record of all my courses. I draw a fence by fence record of what

happened. I have kept detailed statistics of other people's courses too. I have the records of all the Olympic courses since 1924 at home. I also have all the Olympics since 1948 on film. I look at them repeatedly. I study the evolution of show jumping. Before I build I always watch the warm up classes, it is so important for me to know how the horses are jumping when they come to a show or a championship. I look at the footing and how the horses react to it. You have to know whether the ground is in favour of the horses or not. If the footing doesn't help I have got to compensate for it. I incorporate more technical subtleties. Distances that encourage the rider to think and to know what his horse is capable of doing. By knowing your horse you can maximise your chances. One year I said to Bert de Nemethy that a related distance was rather long. He replied,"Oh no, that's not a real problem, instead of riding a tempo of 350m/s you'll have to increase your tempo to 380m/s. This way the horse's stride will lengthen." His remark made a big impression on me. I thought, yes I want to achieve this, ride a higher tempo and have the horse extend automatically.

'Of course I also happen to build rubbish at times, in which case I have to admit it and make sure that it will never happen again. The riders and all those involved have to forgive me and they can be sure that I will never repeat the same mistake. On the other hand, sometimes riders think it is impossible to jump a certain fence. When I am convinced that it is possible I will prove it to them.

'Normally I have some 110 fences that I can take to Zurich, Geneva, St Gallen and play around with them. At the 1993 Volvo World Cup Final in Gothenburg I arrived almost like an alien and had to build with limited material. Then I didn't build the warm up classes, Roland Nilsson built those. It makes it difficult to get a feel for it. Yes, you do watch how the horses go, but you have less time to test your own ideas. I did try to incorporate new things over the days, I pulled all the plugs but I found it almost impossible to create something innovative. I would have loved to get two or three new things in there to freshen the whole thing up a touch, and to make it more interesting for the public too.

'I am a person who has to work under pressure otherwise nothing surfaces. I am not creative when I plan my courses too much in advance and more importantly there are so many things that I have to consider such as the quality of the horses that are taking part.

'Harmony is important for me. Strangely enough, if you have a class where riders get to choose their own line, you'd be surprised what crazy lines they actually come up with, it is anything but harmonious or rhythmical! When I walk a course, I want to create a rhythm. Now, if a rider cuts it to pieces, I can hardly take the blame.

'Horses and riders have to be in far better physical condition indoors than outdoors. It is a different technique and the course designer has to bear that in mind too. When I hold seminars, I always tell people who want to build more and more technical courses that you have got to think about the horses too. They have to recuperate and breathe too. Especially indoors where the air quality isn't very good. This draws on the horse's condition. Outdoors, courses might be longer, up to 1000 metres but horses have 50 or 100 metres to catch their breath.

'I want to stay fresh, have time to look around, gather ideas from various places so to find creativity. There is always the danger of falling into a pattern and it would be like feeding ideas into a computer and the computer could spit out various courses. I want to be creative. This is why I build my own fences at home or give instructions to build fences to my specifications.

'I would like to build the Volvo World Cup Final in Geneva. It is not so much the European Championships or the Olympics I am after but Geneva would be nice. The arena is huge and I could bring my own material. This would give me the opportunity to play around and have fun.'

HORSES AND RIDERS

Show jumping is at its best when horses and riders tackle the most difficult fence sequences with seeming ease and elegance. It is at its best when riders show control but not dominance over the animal. It is wonderful to watch how a rider adjusts to the horse's natural rhythm, letting the horse move in a free flowing motion. The horse, whose origin embodies nature, and the human who is governed by a highly developed intellect. Horses exude power: a force so superior to human strength. A spirit so free and unspoiled. Show jumping brings the two together. Furthermore, it forms a partnership consisting of two performers who metamorphose into one: knowledge and intuition on behalf of the rider, together with the willingness to cooperate on behalf of the horse. A willingness that has emerged out of a mutual understanding and trust. This chapter shows what can be achieved when such horses and riders work together.

When photographing, I want to capture all of what show jumping means in a single shot. Not an easy assignment because of the complexity of the sport. However, an action packed shot can hold all the excitement of the moment. A tightly framed shot can show the rider's expression and enhance the difficulty he or she might have encountered while performing. On the other hand it can also amaze the viewer by showing with what ease a demanding task has been executed. A wider framed shot shows more of the course, such as dimensions and designs of the fences. Those pictures might not hold as much drama as the tightly framed ones, but they allow us to get a full view as well as a feeling for what it is that horses and riders are tackling.

It is rewarding to freeze the motion over the fence which will show the horse off at his very best. The style in which he jumps, knees under his chin so to speak. This moment is also the one the riders like to see the most! It shows them what a 'trier' their horse is. It proves to them that their partners are really giving everything. But if you only show horses in that particular phase, the spectrum would be incomplete and the images all the same.

Some horses such as Milton or Helena Weinberg's Just Malone show a unique technique from the back end. All horses differ slightly in their styles. Not only when jumping but also when approaching a fence. I like to try and capture the individuality of each. Photographs allow you to reflect on such moments, for example, Milton will always put one ear back on the last stride before take off and on the downward action of jumping. This is a sign that he is listening to John at the same time as he is concentrating on the question that lies ahead.

AT THE OLYMPICS IN BARCELONA 1992, ANNE KURSINSKI (USA) AND CANNONBALL WERE THE FIRST TO GO FOR THE US TEAM. THEY WERE ELIMINATED IN THE FIRST ROUND BUT DISPLAYED ENORMOUS DETERMINATION TO FINISH THE SECOND WITH ONLY ONE FENCE DOWN, WHICH HELPED THE US TEAM TO FIFTH PLACE.
'WE JUST HAD TO MAKE IT AROUND! HE WAS VERY GREEN FOR THE OLYMPICS. I HAD TO CONVINCE HIM THAT HE WAS ABLE TO DO IT — HE DIDN'T BELIEVE IN HIMSELF AND BACKED OFF THE HUGE JUMPS AND THEIR BARENESS. I WOULD DESCRIBE CANNONBALL AS A LITTLE RED HEAD! HE IS LIKE A PONY: COCKY AND NOT TOTALLY TRUSTWORTHY. HE IS EXTREMELY TALENTED AND TEMPERAMENTAL — I LOVE HIM A LOT. WHEN HE IS ON MY SIDE WHEN WE WORK AS A TEAM THEN WE ARE FABULOUS'

People often ask me whether I use a motor drive and keep my finger on the shutter during the whole jumping motion to achieve the desired image The answer is simply no. If you apply that technique, you can be sure that you will get a lovely sequence of all the unwanted phases! A motor driven camera is, however, very handy because it means that you can keep looking through the camera without having to bring it away from your eye to wind it on to the next frame. You can therefore follow horse and rider with the option to release the shutter whenever you think it worthwhile. Yes, of course a motor driven camera does offer you the possibility of recording a sequence, but one has to develop a feel for it just as accurately as one has to get a feeling for that single frame. It is a matter of timing. On the high-speed mode a top camera will shoot up to five frames per second. This again depends on how full your power supply is. On a fast mode the batteries get literally eaten up in no time. When the batteries loose juice, the performance of the motor drive diminishes and you have to adjust to it. While shooting, you notice how powerful your equipment is by the noise it makes. Over the years, I have acquired an acute ear for my motor drive.

VALUED TEAM MEMBERS — WILLI MELLIGER OF SWITZERLAND AND PORTER AT SPRUCE MEADOWS, CALGARY 1989, WHERE THE TEAM PLACED SECOND.
'I ONLY RODE PORTER FOR SIX MONTHS. THOMAS FRÜHMANN AND WALTER GABATHULER RODE HIM BEFORE. HE HAD DONE GREAT THINGS WITH THOMAS. WE WON A FEW GOOD CLASSES TOO. HE ALWAYS GAVE ME A GREAT FEELING, BUT HE WAS DIFFICULT TO RIDE. ONE HAD TO UNDERSTAND HIM. HE WENT VERY WELL IN CALGARY, WE STAYED CLEAR IN THE FIRST ROUND AND HAD FOUR FAULTS IN THE SECOND ROUND OF THE NATIONS CUP'

Other horses will have both ears pricked well-forward when approaching. Others will have both ears folded back when jumping. All of this is captured on film and can help to understand the horse's disposition. The individuality of the horse's character can be recorded in a split second.

There are some segments of the horse's motion over a fence that when photographed look misleading: taken too early on the upwards movement, it can give the impression that the horse had the front rail down; too late usually results in a picture that shows a horse hanging over a fence, with his forelegs half unfolded. This does not show the horse off at his very best. I dislike these shots and when they happen, they go in the bin straight away! Luckily pictures like that don't occur too often.

Another important factor that comes with experience is remembering the various styles the riders adopt when in mid-air. Some duck to the left others to the right. The ones I like most are those who stay right in the middle, looking over the horse's neck onto the next fence, as they have been taught! It just makes life so much easier because you can catch them from either side. I can't recall how many pictures land in the bin after each show simply because the shots resemble unidentified flying objects. After all the riders expressions are important. Some riders, and John Whitaker is a specialist, alternate sides. With him, you never can tell to which side he will duck. One normally tries to anticipate the side that the riders will favour by looking at the line of the course. If the next fence in line goes to the right, the chances are that the rider will have his head on the right, in anticipation of the next fence. With John you can never be sure! He is such an intuitive and natural rider that he probably couldn't even tell you himself where he leans when jumping. When he is riding Milton, the chances of a good photograph are even slimmer because Milton doesn't like having his mane plaited, which means that his mane often gets thrown up when he jumps, covering John's face. It is something of an extra challenge to get a decent shot of the two!

German riders like Franke Sloothaak, Otto Becker or Ludger Beerbaum are a dream to photograph. They have never let me down so far. They sit bang in the middle looking out straight through the horse's ears. So I suddenly found myself wanting the riders with the best style to win purely because I have good shots of them and the published photographs will definitely show how wonderful their achievement was. I cannot be totally objective when on a job. I have my favourites. But it doesn't stop there, I admire so many riders and want them to do well, because, together with the horses they ride,

AVONTUUR IS A BELGIUM WARMBLOOD STALLION BY JASPER AND COVERS 50—60 MARES A YEAR. HERE HE IS RIDDEN BY JC VANGEENBERGHE OF BELGIUM AT THE PIAZZA DI SIENA CSIO, ROME 1990.
'THIS PICTURE BRINGS BACK MIXED FEELINGS BECAUSE IT WAS AFTER THE SHOW IN ROME THAT EVERYTHING SEEMED TO FALL APART WITH AVONTUUR AND I HAD TO PUT HIM AWAY FOR A YEAR . . . IT'S A WONDERFUL PICTURE, THE BEST I HAVE SEEN OF A HORSE JUMPING. HE IS JUMPING BRILLIANTLY, HE PULLS HIS SHOULDERS HIGH UP, HIS LEGS ARE LEVEL, HIS EARS ARE PRICKED. HE IS AN EASY WINNER, EXTREMELY CAREFUL. THIS PICTURE SHOWS THE CAPABILITY OF THE HORSE, THE AVONTUUR THAT YOU WILL SEE ON THE CIRCUIT AGAIN'

they simply demonstrate such accomplished horsemanship. My emotions often get the better of me, and I let off steam when I miss a shot.

The selection in this chapter was made by looking at the essence of the shot itself rather than choosing a particular rider or horse. It was hard to establish what makes an interesting image. The criteria was to demonstrate the diversity of show jumping.

(ABOVE) SHINING EXAMPLE WAS A REAL FAMILY HORSE THAT HAS NOT ONLY WON NUMEROUS CLASSES FOR HARVEY SMITH BUT ALSO FOR SONS ROBERT AND STEVEN. HERE ARE HARVEY AND 'NORMAN' AS HE WAS NICKNAMED, AT THE DERBY MEETING, HICKSTEAD 1986. 'SHINING EXAMPLE WAS A GOOD FINE HORSE. HE COULD BEAT ANY HORSE IN THE WORLD ON HIS DAY. FOR TWO SEASONS HE DIDN'T COME HOME FROM A SHOW WITHOUT HAVING WON AT LEAST TWO CLASSES THERE. HE WAS QUITE UNIQUE, HE COULD WIN SPEED CLASSES, GRAND PRIX AND THE DERBY ALL AT THE SAME MEETING. YOU COULD GO RIGHT THROUGH THE CARD AND WIN THEM ALL! HE WAS A BIG HORSE WITH A HUGE AMOUNT OF TALENT. HE WAS VERY VERY QUICK. WHERE OTHER HORSES TOOK FOUR STRIDES, HE WOULD DO IT IN THREE. HE WAS DIFFICULT TO RIDE AT FIRST BUT I GOT HIM GOING WELL'

KILCOLTRIM, VERSATILE IN BOTH GRAND PRIX AND PUISSANCE, COMPETED WITH CAPT JOHN LEDDINGHAM AT THE PIAZZA DI SIENA ROME 1990. BETWEEN 1986 AND 1989, THE DUO WON FOUR CONSECUTIVE PUISSANCES AT THE ROYAL DUBLIN HORSE SHOW.
'ROME IS A FABULOUS SHOW WITH A UNIQUE SETTING — MY FAVOURITE PLACE NEXT TO RIDING IN FRONT OF THE HOME CROWD IN DUBLIN. KILCOLTRIM WAS MY TICKET TO THE SEOUL OLYMPICS. HE DIDN'T LIKE THE FOOTING THERE BUT I HAD A GREAT TIME! HE HAD A TRICKY TEMPERAMENT. HE WAS A FABULOUS HORSE TO RUN TO A BIG WALL WITH. I HAD TOTAL TRUST IN HIM. HIS BRAVERY WAS AMAZING. HE WAS NEARLY TOO BRAVE THEREFORE NOT REALLY CAREFUL ENOUGH FOR 14 FENCES IN A GP. I BOUGHT HIM TOGETHER WITH THE ARMY. UNFORTUNATELY HE HAD A BAD LUNG INFECTION AND HE HAD TO BE PUT DOWN . . . WHENEVER I THINK OF HIM I REMEMBER HIS ENORMOUS SCOPE AND HIS LOVELY BRIGHT OUTLOOK ON LIFE'

DAVID BROOME AND
COUNTRYMAN CAME THIRD IN
THE GP AT THE 1992 RIHS,
HICKSTEAD. COUNTRYMAN IS
IRISH, A HALF BROTHER TO
MONSANTA, AND COMES FROM
FRANK KERNAN'S YARD. THE
PAIR'S GREATEST
ACHIEVEMENT WAS COMING
EQUAL FOURTH IN THE
INDIVIDUAL CONTEST AT THE
1988 SEOUL OLYMPICS.
'COUNTRYMAN IS VERY NICE
TO RIDE, BUT HE NEEDS A FAIR
BIT OF WORK BEFORE CLASSES.
I HAVE TO GET HIM WORKING
ABSOLUTELY RIGHT. HE HAS
GOT A LOVELY EVEN STRIDE
AND HE IS LOVELY TO DO
DISTANCES ON. HE IS TERRIBLY
QUICK OFF THE MARK WHEN
YOU WANT TO MAKE A MOVE.
HE JUMPS BETTER OUT OF A
RHYTHM SO I CAN'T REALLY
PUSH HIM TOO MUCH AGAINST
THE CLOCK. HE HAS GOT A
REALLY HARD CHARACTER, IT
TOOK MORE THAN SIX MONTHS
TO BREAK HIM IN. HE IS AS
TOUGH AS OLD NAILS! WHAT I
LIKE MOST ABOUT HIM IS THE
WAY HE COMES OFF THE
FLOOR. HE HAS GOT A LOT OF
POWER. HE IS VERY HONEST.
HE LOOKS AFTER AN OLD MAN
PRETTY WELL'

(BELOW) THE SMALL GRAND PRIX AT THE 1991 CSIO ROTTERDAM: HERVÉ GODIGNON AND LA BELLETIERE ARE COMING ROUND THE CORNER ABOUT TO TACKLE A FENCE. ROTTERDAM HAS ALWAYS BEEN A FRUITFUL PLACE FOR HERVÉ AND LA BELLETIERE.

'MY YEARS WITH LA BELLETIERE HAVE BEEN SEVEN YEARS OF MARRIAGE, OF STRESSFUL MARRIAGE AT TIMES BECAUSE SHE WASN'T EASY. WE BOTH HAD TO WORK AT IT. WE BECAME A VERY GOOD COUPLE. MY CAREER RESTARTED WITH LA BELLETIERE. SHE BROUGHT ME ENORMOUS JOY, ENORMOUS SATISFACTION AND MANY VICTORIES. LAST YEAR SHE STILL WON THREE OR FOUR BIG GRAND PRIX, LIKE DAUVILLE AND BETUNE. SHE DEFINITELY REPRESENTS A BIG PART OF MY LIFE.

'A LIFE WITH ALL ITS UPS AND DOWNS, ITS DECEPTIONS AND ITS INTENSE PLEASURES. LA BELLETIERE IS 16 AND I AM THINKING OF RETIRING HER AT THE END OF THIS YEAR, SHE DESERVES A REST, AND I BELIEVE THAT ONE SHOULD RETIRE A HORSE BEFORE THEY START TO DECLINE.

SHE IS A VERY STRONG-WILLED MARE, VERY TEMPERAMENTAL — DIFFICULT TO CONTROL. SHE CAN PUT HERSELF IN A LOT OF TROUBLE, BUT AT THE SAME TIME SHE IS ALSO CAPABLE OF GETTING HERSELF OUT OF IMPOSSIBLE SITUATIONS THANKS TO HER NERVOUS INPUT. THIS IS MAYBE A WEAKNESS BUT AT THE SAME TIME IT REPRESENTS HER QUALITIES. I WOULD DESCRIBE HER AS THE BLACK DEVIL'

JAPPELOUP'S LAST BIG OUTING BEFORE HIS RETIREMENT AT THE 1991 CALGARY CSIO IN SPRUCE MEADOWS. HIS PERFORMANCE WAS AS BRILLIANT AS USUAL. PIERRE DURAND STILL FEELS THE LOSS OF HIS BELOVED HORSE.

'FOR ME, CALGARY 1991 WILL ALWAYS BE A FORMIDABLE MEMORY FILLED WITH GREAT EMOTIONS BECAUSE IT WAS JAPPELOUP'S LAST APPEARANCE AT THE HIGHEST LEVEL OF THE SPORT. JAPPELOUP HANDLED IT SO WELL. HE WAS STILL RUBBING SHOULDERS WITH THE BEST HORSES IN THE WORLD. I WAS OVERCOME WITH JOY BY IT. ALTHOUGH I KNEW THAT I WANTED TO RETIRE HIM WHEN HE WAS STILL AT HIS BEST AND KNOWING THAT I HAD SET THE DATE FOR 1991, HIS PERFORMANCE MADE ME THINK WHETHER THE TIME WAS ACTUALLY RIGHT. I WAS IN A DILEMMA BUT DEEP DOWN I KNEW THAT I HAD TO RETIRE HIM WHILE HE WAS STILL GIVING HIS RIVALS A RUN FOR THEIR MONEY. CARRYING THE DAY OUT THE WAY HE DID, MADE ME BELIEVE THAT JAPPELOUP MUST HAVE KNOWN THAT THIS WAS GOING TO BE HIS LAST TURN OUT AND SO HE FELT LIKE LEAVING HIS COMPETITORS IN STYLE'

THE 1992 RIHS HELD AT
HICKSTEAD: JOHN WHITAKER
AND MILTON PLACED SECOND
BEHIND TIM GRUBB AND
DENIZEN IN THE OLYMPIC
TRIALS.

'HICKSTEAD IS THE BEST SHOW
IN ENGLAND. IF HORSES GO
WELL AT HICKSTEAD, THEY'LL
GO WELL EVERYWHERE. IT'S A
GOOD PLACE FOR US TO FIND
OUT HOW GOOD YOUR HORSE
REALLY IS. IT'S AN IMPRESSIVE
PLACE. I REMEMBER MY FIRST
TIME IN THE MAIN ARENA VERY
WELL. I WAS 13 AND RODE IN
THE JUNIOR FOXHUNTER FINAL.
IT WAS A BIT OF A FRIGHTENING
MOMENT. BY THE TIME I BECAME
SENIOR, I WAS A BIT MORE USED
TO IT. AS FOR MILTON, HE GOES
REALLY WELL AT HICKSTEAD. HE
PUTS A LOT INTO IT. HE SEEMS
TO LIKE IT BECAUSE OF THE BIG
SOLID FENCES'

THIS DUO, HUGO SIMON AND APRICOT D, WON A SILVER MEDAL FOR AUSTRIA DURING THE OLYMPICS IN
BARCELONA 1992.
'LOOKING AT THIS PICTURE, I CAN SEE EVERYTHING THAT WE HAVE EXPERIENCED AND ALL WE HAVE LIVED
THROUGH. IT REVEALS THE READINESS FOR BATTLE AND SUMS UP THE ATTITUDE THAT THE WHOLE TEAM HAD
IN BARCELONA! APRICOT D GAVE ALL HE HAD DURING THE TEAM EVENT! HE HAS ALL THE QUALITIES A SHOW
JUMPER SHOULD HAVE: HE HAS A BALANCED MIND IN THE RING HE IS A GREAT FIGHTER, HE ALWAYS WANTS
TO WIN'

EMMA-JANE BROWN'S FIRST VISIT TO AACHEN 1990 WITH GRINGO, SAW
THEM PLACED SEVENTH IN A SPEED CLASS. THE PAIR HAVE COMPETED
IN NATIONS CUPS, PUISSANCES, SPEED AND GRAND PRIX EVENTS. THAT
YEAR EMMA ALSO RODE HER MARE OYSTER IN THE NATIONS CUP, HER
SCORE OF ONE DOWN IN THE FIRST AND A CLEAR IN THE SECOND
ROUND HELPED THE TEAM TO THIRD PLACE.
'IT WAS A GREAT PLEASURE TO HAVE BEEN SELECTED TO GO TO
AACHEN! I REMEMBER GOING THROUGH THE LAKE . . . IT SEEMED LIKE I
WAS IN THE WATER FOREVER BECAUSE GRINGO WOULD JUST NOT
GALLOP! NORMALLY HE TAKES A HOLD VERY BRAVELY AND NOTHING
SEEMS TO WORRY HIM. BUT BECAUSE HE HAD NEVER BEEN THROUGH
WATER, HE WAS VERY WARY OF WHAT HE SHOULD BE DOING. I FOUND
MYSELF KICKING INSTEAD OF BEING OUT OF CONTROL AND PULLING HIM
BACK AS I USUALLY HAVE TO DO.
GRINGO IS VERY STRONG — HE'S LIKE ARNOLD SCHWARZENEGGER —
HE'LL ALWAYS BE BACK'

GERMAN BRED CORSO AND SWITERLAND'S WILLI MELLIGER DURING THE GP OF AACHEN 1989. THE PARTNERSHIP WON A TEAM BRONZE MEDAL AT THE EUROPEAN CHAMPIONSHIP OF 1987 IN ST GALLEN AS WELL AS BECOMING NATIONAL CHAMPION THE SAME YEAR.

'CORSO WAS AN EXCEPTIONAL HORSE. HE WAS FANTASTIC AS AN EIGHT- AND NINE-YEAR OLD, SO COOPERATIVE WITH A GREAT WILL TO WIN. BUT HE ALWAYS OVER JUMPED HALF A METRE TOO HIGH AND BECAUSE OF HIS WEIGHT, IT CAUSED HIM PROBLEMS ON LANDING, IT GOT TOO MUCH FOR HIS LEGS. HE IS IN RETIREMENT IN IRELAND NOW WITH THE GROOM WHO TOOK CARE OF HIM THEN. I MISS HIM, HE WAS REALLY ONE OF MY BEST HORSES EVER'

ROME'S PIAZZA DI SIENA WAS HOME FOR THE 1990 CSIO WHERE OTTO BECKER AND BENJAMIN TURNED OUT. THEY ONLY SHOWED ON THE CIRCUIT FOR SIX MONTHS. THEIR BEST RESULT HAD BEEN A SECOND PLACE AT THE HAMBURG DERBY.

'I AM TRYING TO TIGHTEN BENJAMIN UP BEFORE TAKE OFF. I AM SITTING WELL INTO HIM, TRYING TO INFLUENCE HIS PERFORMANCE OVER THE JUMP. HE IS VERY ATTENTIVE, EARS PRICKED, VERY CONCENTRATED. HE ALWAYS GAVE HIS BEST. IN THE PICTURE HE ACTUALLY REMINDS ME OF A PANTHER; VERY ALERT, LOOKING STRAIGHT AHEAD, LIKE STALKING HIS PREY, IN THIS CASE THE FENCE WHICH HE IS ABOUT TO ATTACK'

PAUL DARRAGH (IRE) AND KILLELEA CLOCKED UP THE FASTEST JUMP OFF BY FAR, BUT HAD A FENCE DOWN AT THE KING GEORGE V GOLD CUP, HICKSTEAD. THE IRISH THOROUGHBRED HAD BEEN WITH PAUL SINCE AUGUST 1990. THEY FORMED A TEAM IN NO TIME WINNING THE FRANKFURT AND OSLO GRAND PRIX THE SAME YEAR. IN 1991 THEY WON THE GRAND PRIX OF THE RIHS. PAUL AND KILLELEA USED THE TWO HICKSTEAD MEETINGS OF 1992 AS A BUILD UP FOR THE BARCELONA OLYMPICS. SADLY KILLELEA DIED ON HIS WAY BACK FROM BARCELONA.

'KILLELEA WAS A VERY GOOD HICKSTEAD HORSE. WE WERE RATHER UNLUCKY NOT TO WIN THE KING GEORGE V GOLD CUP. HE STOOD AT 17.3HH AND HAD A LOVELY BOLD STRIDE, A LOVELY WAY TO GO. HE WASN'T A BIG POWER JUMPER, HE JUMPED FROM HIS PACE. HE WAS VERY FAST, HE WOULD EAT UP THE GROUND. A FUN HORSE TO WORK WITH. HIS STYLE WAS SLIGHTLY UNORTHODOX. HE HAD A FUNNY WAY OF USING HIS BACK END, BUT I THOUGHT THAT IT WAS BETTER TO LEAVE HIM COMFORTABLE RATHER THAN TO CHANGE HIM. I LET HIM DO HIS OWN THING. HE WAS A VERY INTELLIGENT HORSE; BEING A THOROUGHBRED HE GOT STRESSED VERY EASILY AND ONE HAD TO RECOGNIZE IT. HE WAS NEARLY AN IDEAL HORSE. HE TRIED TO LEAVE THE RAILS UP'

THE WORLD EQUESTRIAN GAMES, STOCKHOLM 1990: MARIA GRETZER OF SWEDEN AND MARCOVILLE PLACED 35TH IN THE INDIVIDUAL, AND NINTH WITH THE TEAM.

'STOCKHOLM WAS OUR FIRST REALLY BIG SHOW, OUR FIRST CHAMPIONSHIP. IT WAS A GREAT FEELING TO REALISE THAT I COULD GO OVER THESE HUGE FENCES WITH MARCOVILLE! I LOVE RIDING IN FRONT OF MY HOME CROWD. I HAVE RIDDEN MORE GOOD COURSES THAN BAD ONES IN MY HOME COUNTRY. MARCOVILLE IS A VERY NERVOUS MARE. IT DOESN'T REALLY SHOW BUT THIS IS WHY I CANNOT PUSH HER AGAINST THE CLOCK. BUT SHE IS TOUGH AND IT IS WONDERFUL TO KNOW THAT YOU ARE SITTING ON A HORSE THAT CAN JUMP ANY COURSE IN THE WORLD'

(ABOVE) THOMAS FRÜHMANN (AUSTRIA) AND GENIUS IN BARCELONA DURING THE 1992 OLYMPICS. THE PAIR SCORED A DOUBLE CLEAR ROUND TO HELP AUSTRIA WIN THE OLYMPIC TEAM SILVER MEDAL. THEY PLACED 21ST IN THE INDIVIDUAL CONTEST.

'GENIUS IS A TYPICAL CHAMPIONSHIP HORSE BECAUSE ONE CAN GET HIM READY FOR DAY X. HE WON'T WIN A GP SERIES LIKE GRANDEUR DID FOR EXAMPLE. HE IS A RATHER NERVOUS HORSE. I HAD A FALL WITH HIM IN AACHEN AND THERE WAS HARDLY ANY TIME TO TRAIN BEFORE BARCELONA. IT WAS LUCKY THAT THE TEAM EVENT WAS HELD BEFORE THE INDIVIDUAL CONTEST BECAUSE HE WOULD NOT HAVE COPED WITH THE CLIMATE. HE WASN'T REALLY ALL THAT FIT BUT GAVE ALL HE HAD FOR THE TEAM EVENT. YOU HAVE TO SAVE HIM, YOU CAN'T GO FLAT OUT EVERY DAY. HE IS RELATIVELY EASY TO RIDE IF YOU CAN HANDLE HIS NERVES. HE HAS A GOOD MOUTH AND HE IS CAREFUL. REALLY HE HAS ALL THE INGREDIENTS OF A CLASS HORSE'

COMPETING IN THE NATIONS CUP ROUND AT THE CSIO 1992 MEETING AT HICKSTEAD, THIS WAS RENÉ TEBBLE'S SECOND TIME IN HICKSTEAD. ALEX HAD NEVER BEEN TO THIS IMPRESSIVE ARENA BEFORE, AND THE TWO HAD ONLY BEEN TOGETHER FOR FOUR WEEKS PRIOR TO COMPETING HERE.

'I KNEW THAT ALEX HAD A PROBLEM WITH WATER JUMPS BEFORE COMING TO HICKSTEAD . . . BUT IN THE GRAND PRIX WHEN WE JUMPED THE WATER FACING THE EXIT, HE WAS OK, SO WE DECIDED TO PUT HIM IN THE NATIONS CUP. THIS TIME THE WATER HAD TO BE JUMPED IN THE OTHER DIRECTION AND ALEX SIMPLY DIDN'T WANT TO GO NEAR IT! ALEX IS A VERY CRAFTY HORSE, DIFFICULT OUTDOORS BECAUSE HE SPOOKS A LOT. HE KNOWS EXACTLY WHAT HE WANTS AND REALLY NEEDS A STRONG RIDER ON TOP TO PROVE WHO IS THE BOSS'

THE WEATHER HAD BEEN SO BAD AT THE 1990 CSIO AACHEN, THAT THE FIRST COUPLE OF DAYS WERE HELD INDOORS. ALTHOUGH CONDITIONS IMPROVED THE GROUND WAS STILL VERY HEAVY. SPAIN'S LUIS ALVAREZ CERVERA AND MIRAGE MEXICAN HAD ONLY ONE FENCE DOWN, BUT THE SPANISH TEAM DID NOT MAKE IT TO THE SECOND ROUND.

'MIRAGE MEXICAN PUT EVERYTHING HE HAD INTO HIS JOB. HE WAS ALL HEART AND NO SCOPE. HE WASN'T THE MOST CAREFUL OF HORSES. HE WASN'T REALLY A GRAND PRIX HORSE. I FELT A LOT FOR HIM BECAUSE OF HIS BRAVENESS. HE ALWAYS WANTED TO GET ON THE OTHER SIDE OF THE FENCE. NORMALLY HE SHOULD HAVE BEEN COMFORTABLE IN 1.40M COURSES, BUT BECAUSE OF HIS TREMENDOUS HEART, HE WAS ABLE TO HANDLE GRAND PRIX COURSES'

COLEEN BROOK (AUS) AND MERIDIAN DURING THE GRAND PRIX OF THE 1992 CSIO HICKSTEAD. THEY FAULTED TWICE ON THE COURSE, ONCE AT THE WATER.

'HICKSTEAD IS VERY FAMOUS PLACE FOR AN AUSTRALIAN TO COMPETE AT. IT WAS A WONDERFUL EXPERIENCE. THERE IS NO OTHER PLACE LIKE IT. YOU HAVE TO RIDE DIFFERENTLY THERE BECAUSE OF THE GRADIENT OF THE GROUND AND THE SIZE OF THE ARENA.

'I WAS VERY PLEASED WITH MERIDIAN. HE COPED VERY WELL IN THE GRAND PRIX CONSIDERING THAT IT WAS ONLY HIS SECOND TIME IN THE INTERNATIONAL ARENA. HE HAD NEVER SEEN ANYTHING LIKE IT BEFORE. IT WAS MY MISTAKE AT THE WATER JUMP. I DIDN'T GET MOVING EARLY ENOUGH TO GIVE HIM SUFFICIENT TIME TO GET HIS MOMENTUM, SO WE HIT THE TAPE.

'MERIDIAN IS NOT VERY PERSON FRIENDLY. HE IS A VERY GOOD THINKER IN THE RING. NOT DIFFICULT TO RIDE. I STARTED HIM OFF FROM THE RACE TRACK. HE WAS EASY RIGHT FROM THE BEGINNING. HE IS NEAT AND SHARP — YOU DON'T HAVE TO DO THE THINKING FOR HIM — A REAL TRIER'

JENNY ZOER AND WENDELA HAD
ONE FENCE DOWN IN THE FIRST
ROUND OF THE 1990 SPRUCE
MEADOWS DU MAURIER GRAND
PRIX. IT WAS JENNY'S FIRST
APPEARANCE IN CALGARY. THE
PAIR'S BEST RESULT DURING THE
SHOW WAS AN EIGHTH PLACE.
THE PAIR'S BEST ACHIEVEMENT
WAS WHEN WINNING THE GRAND
PRIX AT THE 1992 CSIO MODENA.
THE PAIR BEAT TEAM-MATE, AND
OCCASIONAL TRAINER JOS
LANSINK RIDING EGANO, INTO
SECOND PLACE.
'THE COURSES ARE REALLY BIG
AND DIFFICULT IN CALGARY, BUT
I REALLY LIKE TO RIDE THERE
BECAUSE THE ARENA IS VERY
SPACIOUS. THE ATMOSPHERE IS
SO NICE THERE. THE AUDIENCE IS
SO ENTHUSIASTIC, ESPECIALLY
WHEN RIDERS GO CLEAR.
'I HAVE HAD WENDELA SINCE SHE
WAS SIX-YEARS OLD. SHE WAS IN
FOAL WHEN I GOT HER. I HAD
FIRST SEEN HER IN A FIELD UP IN
THE NORTH OF HOLLAND AND
THEN I SAW A VIDEO OF HER.
SHE LOOKED SO GOOD IN IT
THAT I DECIDED TO TRY HER
OUT. MY FIRST FEELING WAS
THAT SHE WAS EXTRA CAREFUL.
WENDELA HAD A PERFECT
CHARACTER. SHE ALWAYS
JUMPED, SHE WAS VERY
RELIABLE I COULD ALWAYS
COUNT ON HER'

TONY WEBB AND RESERVATION OF
NEW ZEALAND WON THE NZ LEAGUE
OF THE VOLVO WORLD CUP SERIES IN
THE SPRING OF 1990. AFTER THE
1990 WORLD EQUESTRIAN GAMES OF
STOCKHOLM, WHERE THIS PICTURE IS
TAKEN, THE DUO PARTED.
RESERVATION STAYED IN EUROPE, HE
IS PARTLY OWNED BY BRITISH-BASED
BRUCE GOODIN (NZ), AND A
SYNDICATE.
'MY GREATEST SUCCESS WITH
RESERVATION IS COMING SECOND
BEHIND BIG BEN BUT IN FRONT OF
MILTON IN THE DU MAURIER GP
1991 IN CALGARY. RESERVATION IS
HOT TO RIDE. ONE HAS TO TRY AND
SIT VERY QUIETLY ON HIM. HE IS A
BIG SCOPY, HONEST SORT OF
JUMPER. HE WANTS TO BE CAREFUL
BUT SOMETIMES HIS TEMPERAMENT
LETS HIM DOWN. HE LIKES TO
PLEASE. HE IS A SENSITIVE HORSE.
HE IS MUCH BETTER ON BIG SHOW
GROUNDS LIKE HICKSTEAD OR
CALGARY. HE REALLY DOESN'T LIKE
FIBRESAND OR ARTIFICIAL FOOTING
THAT ONE GETS INDOORS. TO SUM
HIM UP I WOULD DESCRIBE HIM AS A
WELL-BROUGHT UP OLD GENTLEMAN'

THE GRAND PRIX OF AACHEN 1988: HELENA WEINBERG (GER) AND JUST MALONE MADE IT TO THE SECOND ROUND BY BEING THE FASTEST FOUR FAULTERS OF THE FIRST ROUND. THEY FINISHED SEVENTH IN THE LINE UP. 'RIDING JUST MALONE WAS LIKE WALKING A TIGHT ROPE. YOU EITHER WENT CLEAR OR IT WAS A DISASTER. HE WAS COMPLETELY UNPREDICTABLE. HE WON THE GRAND PRIX AND WAS DOUBLE CLEAR IN THE NATIONS CUP OF ROME 1990. AT THE NEXT SHOW IN WIESBADEN WE GOT INTO THE RING AND HE STOPPED! HE HAD A VOLATILE CHARACTER. I HAVE NEVER RIDDEN ANOTHER HORSE OF HIS TALENT, YET, I NEVER FELL OFF A HORSE IN THE RING AS MUCH AS I FELL OFF HIM! BUT I ALWAYS BELIEVED IN HIM. HE WAS REALLY BRILLIANT. HIS KICK WAS A SIGN OF EXHUBERENCE, I WISH I HAD ANOTHER LIKE HIM'

AT THE NATIONS CUP OF THE 1989 CSIO HICKSTEAD, JOHAN LENSSENS OF BELGIUM AND DALKIN HAD A SCORE OF ONE IN THE FIRST ROUND, AND TWO FENCES DOWN IN THE SECOND. ALTHOUGH THE BELGIUM TEAM DIDN'T PLACE WELL IN THE COMPETITION, JOHAN STILL HAD A GOOD SHOW PLACING IN A SPEED CLASS. SADLY DALKIN DIED FROM A HEART ATTACK IN 1992.
'HICKSTEAD IS A VERY IMPRESSIVE PLACE. I REMEMBER COMING WITH MY FAMILY. MY FATHER WALKED THE COURSES, HE HAD NEVER SEEN FENCES AS HUGE AS THE ONES IN HICKSTEAD! IT IS ONE OF THE BEST ARENAS IN THE WORLD. I LOVE IT THERE BECAUSE I LIKE TO GALLOP. THERE IS LOTS OF SPACE AND I LIKE THE LONG POLES. BUT YOU REALLY NEED GOOD HORSES TO COMPETE AT HICKSTEAD, ESPECIALLY FAST SPEED HORSES.
'DALKIN HAD A PROBLEM IN THE TRIPLE COMBINATION. I HAD TO RETIRE HIM. HE ALWAYS HAD A PROBLEM MAKING DISTANCES. THE COMBINATION WAS UPHILL AND THE DISTANCES WERE VERY LONG. DALKIN COULDN'T DO IT BECAUSE HE ALWAYS JUMPED TOO HIGH AND NOT FORWARD ENOUGH. HE WAS ALSO VERY SPOOKY BUT I LIKED HIM A LOT. WHEN I FIRST GOT HIM HE WOULDN'T GO NEAR WATER. IT TOOK ME ONE YEAR TO GET HIM USED TO JUMPING WATER. I TOOK HIM AROUND FARMS, JUMPED HIM OVER ALL KINDS OF FUNNY LOOKING FENCES, OUT OF FIELDS. I MADE HIM GO THROUGH WATER. EVEN IF IT TOOK AN HOUR, I NEVER GAVE UP AND FINALLY HE GAVE IN AND TRUSTED ME. WE EVEN WON A DERBY IN BELGIUM. HE WAS FAIRLY EASY TO RIDE AND A VERY POWERFUL HORSE'

(BELOW) JOAN SCHARFFENBERGER (USA) AND DOMINCA, THE GRAND PRIX OF THE 1988 ROTTERDAM CSIO.

'DOMINCA WAS REALLY ALWAYS MY SPEED HORSE. THAT YEAR I HAD TO PUT HER IN THE BIG CLASSES BECAUSE I DIDN'T BRING ANOTHER HORSE TO ROTTERDAM. IT WAS THE FIRST TIME SHE HAD TO JUMP OVER SUCH A BIG TRACK. SHE DID REALLY WELL, SHE ONLY HAD ONE DOWN IN THE GP. SHE IS THE MOST CAREFUL AND THE FASTEST HORSE I HAVE EVER HAD! SHE WON MORE MONEY THAN THE BOYS AND USUALLY PAID FOR THEIR WAY WHEN THEY DIDN'T DO TOO WELL! I AM BREEDING FROM HER NOW AND SHE HAS HAD HER FIRST FOAL. IT LOOKS JUST LIKE HER — WONDERFUL'

THIS WAS THE FIRST APPEARANCE OF JOE TURI (GB) AND VITAL IN AACHEN, 1987. THEY STAYED CLEAR IN THE FIRST ROUND AND HAD ONE FENCE DOWN IN THE SECOND. THE BRITISH TEAM PLACED SECOND AFTER AN EXCITING JUMP OFF AGAINST THE US TEAM. VITAL IS A STALLION, AND COVERS UP TO 40 MARES A YEAR. JOE DOESN'T RIDE HIM ANYMORE, OWNER MICHAEL BULLMAN MANAGES HIS CAREER.

'VITAL WAS ALWAYS LAZY. AS A FOUR-YEAR OLD, HE WAS NEVER EXUBERANT EXCEPT WHEN HE JUMPED OR WHEN YOU TRIED TO GET ON HIM. I ALWAYS NEEDED FOUR PEOPLE TO HELP ME GET ON HIM. I COULDN'T AFFORD TO KEEP SO MANY PEOPLE, SO I GAVE HIM TO JOE TO RIDE BECAUSE HE COULD VAULT ONTO HIM! HE WAS FABULOUS TO RIDE, SO EASY. HE HAS A GREAT PERSONALITY. YOU ALWAYS KNOW THAT WHEN HE PUTS HIS EARS BACK WHEN YOU GO TO PUT THE BRIDLE ON, HE IS IN FIGHTING FORM. HE IS THE SOUNDEST HORSE I HAVE EVER OWNED. I WOULD NEVER EVER SELL HIM'

THIS WAS NIGEL COUPE'S FIRST VISIT TO AACHEN WITH CROSBY; THE PAIR HAD A GREAT SHOW. NOT ONLY DID THEY PLACE FIFTH IN THIS EVENT, THEY ALSO WON ANOTHER SPEED CLASS BEATING THE BEST RIDERS IN THE WORLD. 'TO BE RIDING IN AACHEN IS ABSOLUTELY OUT OF THIS WORLD. IT'S A DREAM COME TRUE, ESPECIALLY WHEN YOU'RE ONLY 19 AT THE TIME. RIDING IN THAT PARTICULAR CLASS, A-ONE-A YEAR CLASS THAT TAKES YOU THROUGH THE LAKE, IS A REAL ADVENTURE — A FANTASTIC FEELING. CROSBY IS MAINLY A SPEED HORSE. HE HAS WON A LOT FOR ME. HE IS BUZZY TO RIDE, REAL EASY ACTUALLY. HE'S GOT A BIG HEART, HE'S VERY VERY FAST AND AT THE END OF THE DAY HE WILL ALWAYS HELP YOU'

(LEFT) THE FIRST ROUND OF THE TEAM EVENT AT THE 1990 WORLD EQUESTRIAN GAMES, STOCKHOLM,
WHERE SWITZERLAND'S PHILIP GUERDAT AND LANCIANO FAULTED AT THE WATER JUMP. LANCIANO HAD A
PROBLEM OF DEHYDRATION BETWEEN THE TWO ROUNDS AND DIDN'T DO WELL IN THE SECOND. THE SWISS
TEAM PLACED SEVENTH.
'THANKS TO LANCIANO I MANAGED TO WIN THE GRAND PRIX AT THE 1988 CSIO IN DINARD. HE WAS A VERY
RELIABLE HORSE. I RODE HIM IN 25 NATIONS CUPS AND HIS WAS NEVER THE DISCARD SCORE. VERY RARELY
DID HE HAVE TWO FENCES DOWN. MIND YOU, HE OFTEN HAD ONE DOWN BUT RARELY TWO! HE WAS A
WILLING HORSE, I HAD A LOT OF PLEASURE IN RIDING HIM'

ROGER YVES BOST (FR) AND NORTON DE RHUYS CAMERA AT THE PIAZZA DI SIENA ROME, IN THE 1990 GRAND
PRIX. 'BOSTY' AND NORTON DE RHUYS WENT ON TO WIN A TEAM GOLD MEDAL AT THE WORLD EQUESTRIAN
GAMES IN STOCKHOLM THE SAME YEAR.
'MY FIRST FEELING IS THAT NORTON DE RHUYS IS THE BEST! CERTAINLY THE BEST HORSE I HAVE RIDDEN SO
FAR. HE HAS A LOT OF ENERGY, HE IS VERY CAREFUL AND WILLING. HE IS COURAGEOUS AND LIKES WINNING
JUST AS MUCH AS I DO'

IRELAND'S EDDIE MACKEN HAS WON THE HICKSTEAD DERBY A RECORD FOUR TIMES IN A ROW IN THE YEARS 1976, 1977, 1978 AND 1979. THE 1986 DERBY WAS FLIGHT'S FIRST AND ONLY ATTEMPT. THE PAIR STAYED CLEAR UP TO THE SECOND LAST FENCE BUT HAD THE LAST COUPLE OF FENCES DOWN.

'FLIGHT WAS THE MOST GENUINE HORSE I HAVE EVER RIDDEN. WHAT HE LACKED IN TALENT HE MADE UP IN HEART. HE WAS LOVELY LOOKING, VERY EASY TO RIDE AND EXTREMELY FOOTSURE. HE ALWAYS PICKED HIS EVERY STEP CAREFULLY. COMING DOWN THE BANK WAS NO PROBLEM WITH HIM. THE ONLY TIME THAT COMING DOWN THE BANK IS A PROBLEM, IS WHEN A HORSE IS NOT CAREFUL ENOUGH.

'ONE THING I'D LIKE TO DO BEFORE I RETIRE IS GO BACK TO HICKSTEAD AND WIN THE DERBY AGAIN'

(RIGHT) MICHAEL WHITAKER (GB) AND GIPFELSTÜRMER, DURING THE JUMP OFF IN A BIG CLASS AT THE CSIO MEETING IN ROME 1990. GIPFELSTÜRMER HAS SINCE RETURNED TO HIS COUNTRY OF ORIGIN, GERMANY, AND FORMED A PARTNERSHIP WITH HOLGER HETZEL.

'GIPFELSTÜRMER IS A REAL TRIER AND REAL GENUINE. HE IS SIMILAR TO MONSANTA, EXTRA CAREFUL AND VERY FAST. HE DOESN'T HAVE A REALLY BIG SCOPE BUT HE CAN STILL JUMP A BIG NATIONS CUP AND A GRAND PRIX. MOST OF ALL HE WAS A REAL WINNER, HE HAS WON A LOT OF CLASSES FOR ME. HE WON TWO CLASSES IN ROME THAT YEAR AND LOOKING AT THE PICTURE, HE MUST HAVE WON THIS ONE'

LUDGER BEERBAUM (GERMANY)
AND ATHLETICO DURING THE GP
IN ROTTERDAM 1991
'WE HAD A GREAT SHOW IN
ROTTERDAM THAT YEAR! HE
LOOKS SO ATTENTIVE! ATHLETICO
CAN DO ANYTHING WHEN HE
PUTS HIS MIND TO IT. THE
PROBLEM IS THAT HE DOESN'T
ALWAYS WANT TO COOPERATE,
TO GIVE EVERYTHING — AS
OPPOSED TO CLASSIC TOUCH OR
RATINA WHO ARE PREPARED TO
GIVE EVERYTHING EVERY DAY.
BUT HE IS A GREAT FIGHTER. HE
IS A BIT OF A GENIUS AND AS IS
OFTEN THE CASE WITH GENIUSES,
THEY DON'T FEEL UP TO
SHOWING THEIR FULL POTENTIAL
EVERY DAY'

GREAT BRITAIN MANAGED TO FIGHT OFF THE CHALLENGE FROM THE IRISH TEAM THAT TOOK THEM ALL THE WAY TO A JUMP OFF. BRITAIN'S EMMA-JANE BROWN AND OYSTER HAD ONE DOWN IN THE FIRST ROUND, STAYED CLEAR IN THE SECOND AND JUMPED THE ALL-IMPORTANT, DECISIVE CLEAR ROUND IN THE JUMP OFF TO TAKE GREAT BRITAIN TO VICTORY.

'RIDING IN A NATIONS CUP IS WONDERFUL. IT IS A GREAT PRIVILEGE. HICKSTEAD IS MY FAVOURITE SHOW ANYWAY AND TO BE IN A TEAM WITH DAVID, MICHAEL AND JOHN MADE ME FEEL VERY PROUD. OYSTER HAS A GREAT DEAL OF SCOPE AND ABILITY. WE HAVE A GREAT PARTNERSHIP. THERE ARE SOME GOOD AND SUCCESSFUL MARES AROUND, SHE IS ONE OF THEM. I CAME ACROSS HER TOGETHER WITH TED EDGAR AT THE END OF A LONG DAY OF LOOKING AT HORSES. WE NEARLY MISSED OUR PLANE BECAUSE I WANTED TO RIDE HER. HER FIRST JUMP WAS VERY GOOD, IT FELT VERY POWERFUL, ESPECIALLY HER BACK END. WHEN YOU GO INTO THE RING YOU KNOW THAT YOU HAVE GOT A LOT OF SCOPE TO BURN. IT IS SO NICE TO HAVE HAD HER AS A YOUNGSTER AND TO HAVE BROUGHT HER ON TO THE TOP LEVEL MYSELF. YOU NEVER KNOW HOW A YOUNGSTER WILL TURN OUT, BUT I CAN HONESTLY SAY THAT OYSTER IS LIKE A DREAM THAT CAME TRUE'

HENK HULZEBOS IS OF DUTCH
ORIGIN AND LIVES IN HOLLAND,
HOWEVER, WITH AUSTRIAN
CITIZENSHIP HE COMPETES FOR
AUSTRIA. WITH A CLEAR FIRST
ROUND, AND SEVEN FAULTS IN THE
SECOND, HENK AND TANGO B
HELPED THE AUSTRIAN TEAM TO
PLACE THIRD IN THE NATIONS CUP
AT THE 1987 CSIO, ROTTERDAM.
HENK GOT TANGO B AS A FIVE-
YEAR OLD AND TOOK HIM
THROUGH THE RANKS TO GRAND
PRIX LEVEL.
'ROTTERDAM IS ONE OF THE NICEST
SHOWS, I'D PUT IT IN SECOND
PLACE, RIGHT BEHIND AACHEN.
THE LOCATION IS SUPERB. A
BEAUTIFUL ARENA UNDER THE
TREES, SET IN A LOVELY FOREST.
THERE IS ALWAYS A FRIENDLY
ATMOSPHERE! TANGO B WAS A
HORSE THAT COULD JUMP
ANYTHING. HE WAS VERY
SENSITIVE, VERY CAREFUL. HE
NEVER LIKED MAKING MISTAKES
AND WHEN HE DID HE USUALLY
GOT SCARED. A FENCE DOWN,
WOULD UPSET HIM FOR THE REST
OF THE COURSE. IN THE NATIONS
CUP THAT YEAR IN ROTTERDAM
FOR EXAMPLE, WE HAD ONE FENCE
DOWN IN THE SECOND ROUND AND
HE GOT FRIGHTENED WHICH
RESULTED IN HIM STOPPING AT
THE NEXT FENCE. HE HAS TO BE IN
THE MOOD FOR THE JOB. HE WAS
DIFFICULT TO RIDE. NOT
EVERYBODY'S CUP OF TEA BUT I
LIKED HIM A LOT'

(LEFT) WITH ONE FENCE DOWN AND A QUARTER OF A TIME FAULT, US RIDER DEBBIE DOLAN AND VIP DID NOT GET INTO THE SECOND ROUND OF THE GRAND PRIX AT THE 1989 CSIO ROME. NEVERTHELESS, DEBBIE HAS GOOD MEMORIES FROM ROME, THE PAIR'S SCORE OF EIGHT AND CLEAR HELPED THE US TEAM TO WIN THE NATIONS CUP.

'JUMPING IN ROME WAS AN OVERWHELMING EXPERIENCE FOR ME. TO BE IN THE COMPANY OF THESE TOP CLASS RIDERS AND TO BE IN A CITY WITH ALL THAT CULTURE AND HISTORY. I DEFINITELY TOOK A WHILE TO ADJUST!

'FOR A STALLION, VIP IS FANTASTIC. NORMALLY STALLIONS DON'T WANT TO HAVE ANYTHING TO DO WITH YOU BUT HE IS A 'PEOPLE' HORSE. HE HAS LITTLE HABITS. HE PLAYS WITH YOU IN THE STABLES. HE LIKES TAKING YOUR KEY RING AND THROWING IT BACK AT YOU. HE IS MORE THAN A HORSE, HE IS MY FRIEND'

GRAND SLAM AND NICK SKELTON TOOK A TEAM BRONZE MEDAL AT THE WORLD EQUESTRIAN GAMES OF 1990 IN STOCKHOLM.

'WHEN I GOT GRAND SLAM AS A FIVE-YEAR OLD, HE DIDN'T HAVE MUCH ABILITY BUT HE WAS VERY CAREFUL AND IMPROVED WITH TIME. HE NEVER HAD A BAD EXPERIENCE, NEVER GOT HURT AND HE NEVER GAVE UP! HE ALWAYS TRIED TO GIVE HIS BEST. HE HAD A LOVELY TEMPERAMENT. HE WAS A SMASHING HORSE TO RIDE. YOU ALWAYS HAD TO BUILD HIS CONFIDENCE UP AT EACH SHOW BY PUTTING HIM IN THE SMALL CLASSES THE FIRST DAY, THEN THE BIGGER ONES AND THEN YOU COULD PUT HIM IN THE GP HE WAS A VERY GENUINE HORSE, EASY TO RIDE, STRAIGHT AND HONEST'

THANKS TO CHIN CHIN'S EFFORTS, THE MEXICAN TEAM CAME THIRD AT THE NATIONS CUP AT THE 1989 MASTERS SPRUCE MEADOWS. RIDER JAIME AZCARRAGA GOT THE HOLSTEIN STALLION AS AN EIGHT-YEAR OLD FROM GERMAN RIDER ACHAX VON BUCHWALD.

'CHIN CHIN IS SUCH A BRAVE HORSE. HE IS REALLY NICE TO RIDE. HE CAN BE A LITTLE DIFFICULT IN HIS MOUTH BUT HE HAS WON SO MUCH FOR ME OVER THE YEARS. WE WON MORE THAN TEN VOLVO WORLD CUP QUALIFIERS IN MEXICO. THANKS TO CHIN CHIN I QUALIFIED THREE TIMES FOR THE VOLVO WORLD CUP FINAL, WINNING THE SOUTH AMERICAN LEAGUE ON ALL THREE OCCASIONS. HIS BEST EVER ACHIEVEMENT WAS WHEN WE PLACED SIXTH IN THE 1988 SEOUL OLYMPICS. HE IS A GREAT HORSE TO HAVE. HE HAS PRODUCED MANY GOOD FOALS. THE ONE I AM THE PROUDEST OF IS THE ONE THAT WON THE INTERNATIONAL FUTURITY STAKES IN THE US. IT WAS THE ONLY CHIN CHIN FOAL AMONGST 300 FOALS THAT CAME OUT THE WINNER. CHIN CHIN IS MY BUDDY AND FRIEND — I LOVE HIM A LOT'

(ABOVE) THE BEST SEASON FOR LUIS ALVAREZ CERVERA OF SPAIN AND MIRAGE MEXICAN WAS 1988. THEY WENT ON TO COMPETE AT THE SEOUL OLYMPICS. AT THE END OF 1990 MIRAGE MEXICAN WAS SOLD TO AN ITALIAN JUNIOR RIDER.

'ROTTERDAM IS A VERY HIGH LEVEL CSIO. I LIKE THE SHOW A LOT. THAT YEAR WE WON THE BIG CLASS ON THE OPENING DAY, BEATING GEORGE MORRIS IN THE JUMP OFF. IT WAS A THRILLING EXPERIENCE FOR ME BECAUSE I NEVER EXPECTED MIRAGE MEXICAN TO REACH THE JUMP OFF LET ALONE WIN THE COMPETITION! THIS WIN TOGETHER WITH A WIN EARLIER IN THE SEASON IN WOLFSBERG, A PRE-AACHEN SHOW, WERE HIS BEST ACHIEVEMENTS. MIRAGE MEXICAN HAD A LOT OF COURAGE BUT NOT QUITE ENOUGH POWER'

THE NATIONS CUP IN AACHEN 1992, WHERE OTTO BECKER AND LUCKY LUKE CONTRIBUTED TO
GERMANY'S VICTORY IN FRONT OF THEIR HOME CROWD.
'AACHEN IS OF COURSE RATHER SPECIAL FOR US GERMANS! I ENJOYED RIDING LUCKY LUKE IN AACHEN
BECAUSE THE COURSES ARE ALWAYS QUITE HIGH THERE AND JUMPING BIG FENCES WAS DEFINITELY
LUCKY LUKE'S STRENGTH. HE COULD JUMP ANYTHING. BUT HE IS A VERY SENSITIVE HORSE. HE HAS A
VERY SLOW CANTER, AND BECAUSE OF HIS SLOW MOVEMENTS, HE DOESN'T HAVE THE BEST
REACTIONS. THIS CAUSED A FEW PROBLEMS LIKE KEEPING WITHIN THE TIME ALLOWED. HE WAS A
VERY FAITHFUL HORSE WHO ALWAYS GAVE HIS BEST. HE WAS VERY CAREFUL IN HIS OWN WAY, A
SAFE HORSE WHO SCORED A LOT OF DOUBLE CLEARS. HIS ASSETS WERE HIS JUMPING ABILITY AND HIS
RELIABILITY. HIS SENSITIVITY MEANT THAT HE WASN'T EASY TO RIDE. ONE HAD TO PUT HIM RIGHT AT
EVERY FENCE'

BRITAIN'S TIM GRUBB LIVES AND
RIDES OUT OF THE AMERICAN
EAST COAST. HE BROUGHT
DENIZEN OVER TO EUROPE IN THE
SPRING OF 1992 HOPING TO
CATCH THE SELECTORS' EYES AND
MAKE THE BRITISH TEAM FOR THE
1992 BARCELONA OLYMPICS. THEY
DID, DENIZEN WAS SEVEN-YEARS
OLD AT THE TIME; THE PAIR
WERE DOING ALRIGHT UP TO THIS
FENCE, BUT FELL ON LANDING
AND RETIRED.
'A WHOLE LOT OF DIFFERENT
THINGS WENT WRONG AT THE
OLYMPICS, STARTING WITH THE
MORNING OF THE EVENT. WHEN I
SCHOOLED DENIZEN, HE SLIPPED
AND FELL IN THE INDOOR ARENA,
BANGED HIMSELF WHICH WASN'T
A GOOD START . . . THE HEAT
DIDN'T HELP, AND HIS SOLES
WERE BURNED FROM THE
FOOTING. THEY HAD MIXED SOME
OIL INTO THE SAND SO THAT IT
WOULDN'T GET TOO DUSTY,
WHICH RESULTED IN A LOT OF
HORSES GETTING SORE FEET. I
BELIEVE THAT THIS WAS ALSO A
PROBLEM FOR DOLLAR GIRL AND
EGANO. WHEN WE CAME TO THIS
FENCE, DENIZEN CAME OFF THE
FRONT RAIL SO WELL AND SO
HIGH, HE COULDN'T BELIEVE HOW
WIDE THE FENCE ACTUALLY WAS
AND JUST COULDN'T MAKE IT. THE
OLYMPICS PROBABLY CAME TOO
EARLY FOR DENIZEN. IT WAS THE
HARDEST COMPETITION HE EVER
HAD TO DO'

THE 1992 CSIO OF SAN MARINO, MODENA IS ALSO KNOWN AS THE PAVAROTTI SHOW, AS IT IS HOSTED BY THE GREAT MAESTRO. HEISMAN DIDN'T DO TOO WELL IN MODENA, BUT HIS RIDER MICHAEL MATZ WON TWO SPEED CLASSES ON OLISCO. THE STALLION HAD BEEN PREVIOUSLY RIDDEN BY FELLOW AMERICAN RODNEY JENKINS. MICHAEL RODE HIM FOR THREE YEARS.

'AFTER THE EFFORTS OF THE OLYMPICS, THE CSIO OF MODENA WAS JUST A LITTLE TOO MUCH FOR HEISMAN. REALLY HE NEEDED A REST BUT THE TEAM HAD TO STAY IN EUROPE FOR QUARANTINE SO I RODE HIM A LITTLE. HEISMAN WAS AN EXCEPTIONAL HORSE. HE COULD BE A LITTLE DIFFICULT IN HIS MOUTH SOMETIMES WHICH WAS THE ONLY THING THAT WOULD BEAT HIM. THIS IS ALSO WHY I GOT INTO TROUBLE AT THE OLYMPICS. HE WAS VERY CONSISTENT DURING OUR OLYMPIC TRIALS. HE HAS WON SEVEN GRANDS PRIX FOR ME'

SECOND BEHIND MILTON CAME
MARK TODD (NZ) AND DOUBLE
TAKE AT HICKSTEAD'S CSIO GP IN
1991.
'HICKSTEAD IS A PREMIER SHOW
JUMPING VENUE. IT IS JUST A
GREAT THRILL TO RIDE IN THE
RING. IT WAS THE FIRST BIG GP
FOR DOUBLE TAKE. I WAS A
LITTLE WORRIED ABOUT HOW HE
WOULD COPE. HE COPED VERY
WELL! HE IS UNIQUE REALLY, NOT
ONLY BECAUSE HE IS A HALF
TROTTER AND HAS AN UNUSUAL
CANTER, WHICH IS VERY
COMFORTABLE ACTUALLY, BUT
BECAUSE HE IS SUCH A STRAIGHT
FORWARD HORSE. HE HAS A
GREAT PERSONALITY. HE CAN BE
A LITTLE CHEEKY IN THE
STABLES, BUT AS LONG AS HE HAS
SOMETHING TO EAT HE IS HAPPY!
HE IS 110% GENUINE'

THE DUTCH TEAM DIDN'T DO AT
ALL WELL AT THE 1992 CSIO
AACHEN; THEY WERE SEVENTH
AFTER THE FIRST ROUND AND DID
NOT QUALIFY FOR ROUND TWO.
PIET RAYMAKERS AND RATINA Z
HAD BOTH ELEMENTS DOWN AT
THE DOUBLE OF WATER DITCHES.
'IT IS A GREAT FEELING TO RIDE
IN THIS ARENA AT AACHEN. YOU
REALLY NEED A SUPER HORSE
LIKE RATINA Z THERE OR ELSE
THE WEEK CAN GET RATHER
LONG.
RATINA Z WAS THE FIRST TOP
HORSE I HAVE EVER HAD. AT FIRST
SHE WAS WILD. SHE HAD THE
SCOPE AND THE QUALITY BUT SHE
WAS DIFFICULT TO CONTROL. I
GOT USED TO HER AND SHE
TRUSTED ME MORE AND MORE
EVERY TIME I WORKED WITH HER.
SHE WAS ALWAYS FIGHTING FOR
ME EVEN WHEN SHE WAS TIRED.
SHE'S A REAL WOMAN. SHE WAS
NEVER AGAINST ME. SHE NEVER
THOUGHT THAT SOMETHING WAS
IMPOSSIBLE; SHE GAVE ME
EVERTHING.'

ANNE KURSINSKI (USA) TOOK
CANNONBALL ON HIS FIRST
OUTING TO AACHEN IN 1991. HIS
FIRST GLIMPSE OF THE COURSE,
THAT TRADITIONALLY LEADS
OVER THE BANK, DITCHES AND
THROUGH THE LAKE, WAS
CLEARLY DAUNTING.
'CANNONBALL HAD WON THE
VERY FIRST SPEED CLASS IN
AACHEN THAT YEAR.
NEVERTHELESS, I WAS
CONCERNED THAT HE MIGHT BE
TOO GREEN FOR THIS PARTICULAR
SPEED CLASS SO I RODE VERY
STRONG TO THE LIVERPOOL.
CANNONBALL REALLY ONLY SAW
THE DITCH IN THE VERY LAST
MOMENT AND LOST HIS HEART.
AT THAT MOMENT I WAS
THINKING, NOW THAT HE REALLY
SCARED HIMSELF BY FALLING
INTO THE HOLE, HOW WILL I
EVER GET HIM OVER IT? WHEN I
RODE DOWN TO IT AGAIN, HE
JUMPED IT FABULOUSLY'

MISHAPS

Immortalizing split seconds of an action is very much a case of being in the right place at the right time. Anticipation based on experience comes into play too. And, like everything we do, a certain amount of luck comes in handy at times. I'd like to point out right from the start that I never go on a shoot to try and find a location where there is bound to be a problem for horses and riders. My main goal is always to photograph horses and riders at their best. I always want to provide evidence of the spectacular manner in which the winning combination has overcome the difficulties of a course. When you are photographing top riders you can be sure that almost all of the fences and questions riders encounter are considerably demanding for them. Anything can happen anywhere. Falls, refusals and mishaps do occur.

I remember that when I first started to photograph equestrian events, I simply couldn't release the shutter if I saw something disturbing through the lens. When I go to a horse trial event, while walking the course I consciously look for a fence that horses will jump in a spectacular manner, showing both the nature of the fence and the effort demanded from horse and rider. I find it interesting to show a horse in full stretch while tackling a drop fence. On one occasion I placed myself at such a

fence; many horses had jumped it beautifully. And I was happy with what I had captured so far. Towards the end of the day, the event was drawing to a close, I was following a competitor through my camera as she was approaching the fence. Suddenly I saw how boldly the horse took off, he stretched out like

AUSTRIA'S THOMAS FRÜHMANN AND CORNADO ON THE OPENING DAY OF THE SPRUCE MEADOWS MASTERS, SEPTEMBER 1990. 'CORNADO WAS A SUPER, SUPER WELL-BEHAVED HORSE. I JUMPED HIM IN ALL SORTS OF CLASSES, AUSTRIAN CHAMPIONSHIP, GRAND PRIX CLASSES, PUISSANCE, SPEED CLASSES AND HE NEVER LOST A SIX-BAR COMPETITION. HE WAS A GREAT HORSE FOR ME. I JUST CANNOT REMEMBER HIM EVER STOPPING FOR ME, BUT WHAT I DO REMEMBER IS THAT IN 1990 THE GROUND AT SPRUCE MEADOWS HAD BEEN VERY BAD ON THE FIRST DAY'

no other horse had done before him. I snapped at that and as I kept following the pair through the lens I witnessed that on landing, the rider was totally out of control, and the horse ran straight into a post and fell very badly. My first reaction was to drop my camera straight away and run to the horse's rescue, which I did. The horse was badly winded, lying on his side and gasping for air. I undid the girth and after a while, he struggled to his feet. The rider was in a state of shock as she realized that her horse had sustained an open leg fracture. It was a tragic moment: the horse's injury was so bad that he had to be put down. A tough photographer might have recorded the whole incident — I couldn't.

I am still not as sharp as other photographers when it comes to pushing that little button at the moment an incident happens. Often I will see that a horse hasn't taken off well and I will not release the shutter. This reaction has made me miss a lot of shots that would have recorded falls or peculiar looking moments.

FINNISH RIDER KATIE HURME AND VANCOUVER TURN OUT FOR THE PRE-CHRISTMAS SHOW OLYMPIA, IN DECEMBER 1990 — A WORLD CUP QUALIFIER. 'VANCOUVER WAS CLEAR UP TO THE SECOND LAST, BUT HAD IT DOWN, THE CROWD WENT "AAAHHH". VANCOUVER GOT SCARED BECAUSE THE FENCES WERE VERY CLOSE TO THE AUDIENCE. THREE STRIDES LATER CAME THE FINAL FENCE BUT HE PUT A FOURTH STRIDE IN AND ALTHOUGH HE WAS FAR TOO CLOSE HE STILL TOOK OFF AND WENT THROUGH THE FENCE . . . SO WE FINISHED WITH EIGHT FAULTS. HE IS A DERBY HORSE REALLY. HE HAS NO SENSE BUT HE ALWAYS WANTS TO GIVE HIS BEST'

In this chapter is a collection of the few shots I did get. They record moments in which something did go wrong. However, I am happy to say that none of the following episodes ended in disaster. When showing the photographs to the riders, I was interested to find out what had gone wrong at the time.

SILVER DUST IS AN IRISH BRED HORSE THAT ROBERT SMITH HALF OWNS. AT THE TIME THIS SEQUENCE WAS TAKEN, AT THE CSIO ROTTERDAM 1991, THE GREY HAD BEEN WITH ROBERT FOR TWO YEARS.

'SILVER DUST DOESN'T STOP NORMALLY . . . HE IS PRETTY GOOD NORMALLY . . . HERE I WAS TOO FAR OFF THE FENCE. IT WASN'T HIS GREATEST WEEK, HE REALLY HAD AN OFF WEEK. HE IS NOT PARTICULARLY EASY. HE IS A FUNNY SORT OF RIDE BECAUSE HE IS SO WIDE. HE CAN BE A LITTLE STRONG SOMETIMES AND RUN OFF WITH YOU A LITTLE. HE IS A REAL POWER HORSE, BUT NOT THE GREATEST OF WINNING HORSES BECAUSE HE IS NOT QUITE QUICK ENOUGH, BUT HE HAS GOT ENOUGH SCOPE. HE IS A LITTLE MAD BUT I LIKED HIM FROM THE BEGINNING AND HE WAS VERY GOOD FROM THE WORD GO. BELIEVE IT OR NOT, HE IS FAIRLY RELIABLE'

DURING A SMALL GRAND PRIX IN ST GALLEN, NOT PART OF THE EUROPEAN CHAMPIONSHIPS, NELSON PESSOA OF BRAZIL AND LASALL STRUGGLED AS LASALL GOT INTO TROUBLE.

'LASALL HAD A PROBLEM IN KEEPING HIS RIGHT FRONT SHOE ON SO WE HAD PUT A STEEL CLIP, WHICH TIGHTENS WITH A SCREW AT THE SIDE, ROUND HIS HOOF. WHEN I WAS WARMING HIM UP I FELT THAT HE WASN'T REALLY RIGHT. HE FELT LAZY BUT I THOUGHT AS THE FOOTING RESEMBLED A POTATO FIELD THAT IT WAS ONLY THE DEEP AND WET GROUND. I TROTTED HIM UP ON EVEN GROUND AND HE SEEMED OK. 'I WAS CALLED DOWN TO THE JUMPING ARENA, ENTERED AND HE STILL FELT LAZY OVER THE FIRST FEW FENCES. THEN CAME FENCE FIVE, THE DOUBLE COMBINATION — THIS SHOT IS THE OUT FENCE. WHEN TAKING OFF HE STARTED RUNNING IN MID-AIR: I SAT BACK, LET GO OF THE REINS TO TRY AND GIVE HIM HIS BALANCE, HE DIDN'T FALL. BY NOW I KNEW THAT HE WAS TRYING TO TELL ME SOMETHING SO I STOPPED. LATER HIS TENDON AND FETLOCK HAD SWOLLEN UP A LOT AND I THOUGHT THAT THE DAMAGE HAD BEEN DONE IN THE COLLECTING RING. A GROOM THAT HAD WORKED FOR ME FOR A LONG TIME WAS THERE. HE POINTED OUT THAT THE STEEL CLIP MIGHT HAVE BEEN TIGHTENED TOO MUCH DENYING THE FOOT ENOUGH BLOOD SUPPLY WHICH RESULTS IN NUMBING THE WHOLE FOOT. WE TOOK THE CLIP OFF IMMEDIATELY AND WITHIN 48 HOURS THE SWELLING WAS GONE. THE POOR HORSE SIMPLY COULDN'T FEEL ANYTHING IN HIS RIGHT FRONT LEG . . . IT ALSO SHOWS HIS BRAVERY, HE ALWAYS TRIED FOR ME'

BELGIAN ERIC WAUTERS GOES
DOWN THE DERBY BANK AT
HICKSTEAD FOR HIS THIRD TIME
IN 1988, BUT IT'S THE VERY FIRST
TIME FOR LITTLE STALLION PRINS
DRUM.
'NEVER BEFORE HAD PRINS DRUM
COME OFF SUCH A HIGH AND
STEEP BANK. HE IS A VERY BRAVE
LITTLE HORSE SO HE JUMPED,
DIVING OFF FROM THE TOP. THE
FEELING WAS STEEP AND QUITE
FAST! I HAD NO TIME TO REALISE
WHAT WAS HAPPENING.
NORMALLY YOU HAVE TO LOOK
FOR CONTROL WHEN YOU ARE
COMING DOWN THE BANK, BUT IN
THIS CASE PRINS DRUM WAS SO
BRAVE THAT HE JUST TOOK MY
HAND AND OFF HE WENT! HE
LANDED ON HIS KNEES AND GOT
UP STRAIGHT AWAY. WE LOST
OUR BALANCE — EVERYTHING!
FINALLY, I DON'T KNOW HOW I
STAYED ON TOP BUT WE
MANAGED TO CARRY ON'

HOPSCOTCH FOUND HIS OWN WAY DOWN THE DERBY
BANK AT HICKSTEAD 1991, AND DIDN'T QUITE
UNSEAT HIS RIDER JOHN WHITAKER:
'HOPSCOTCH GOT HIS HIND LEGS BEHIND HIM AND
COULDN'T STOP HIMSELF, FORTUNATELY HE DIDN'T
COME RIGHT DOWN, HE GOT BACK UP. I WAS LUCKY
TO HAVE STAYED ON TOP. I CIRCLED AND HE JUMPED
THE WHITE RAILS, WE CARRIED ON. IT WAS ONLY
BACK IN THE STABLES WHEN WE TOOK THE BOOTS
OFF THAT WE SAW HE HAD A BIG CUT UNDER HIS
BOOT. LUCKILY IT WASN'T REALLY SERIOUS. I LIKE
HOPSCOTCH A LOT. HE IS SUCH A SOFT HORSE, A
REALLY NICE HORSE TO RIDE. THE KIDS CAN DO
ANYTHING WITH HIM, THEY RIDE HIM AT HOME'

GREAT PARTNERSHIPS

The success of any relationship, whether it is between two people or two creatures of different heritage, works on the same principals. Once we have experienced a definite attraction to one another, we have to try and understand the way our partner's psyche works. Some riders feel immensely drawn to a particular horse. This is an obvious starting point to any relationship. Once a rider has reached a level in which a certain attraction to a particular horse has been established, he moves on to a second level, the level of trying to find out what makes this individual tick. A rider tries to key into the way the horse thinks. He works with the mentality of the horse, and tries to understand the horse's personality, using it to get that bit extra out of the horse.

Some horses, usually the extra special ones, are the ones with a difficult and strong character. A rider who is building up a special relationship with a horse, has to try and work with the difficulties turning them to his advantage. He will find a way of being on the same wavelength as the horse. A partnership will turn into a great one when the two minds, as well as the technical side of understanding a horse's capabilities, meet. As with people a definite chemistry becomes apparent. Two individuals become best friends and have a mutual

respect. But all efforts of understanding don't only come from the rider. The horse tries to understand the rider as well. A great partnership will always benefit from the fact that the horse follows the rider's train of thought.

Furthermore, in a successful partnership, a rider has to know when he has to back off. He has to realise to what degree he can tolerate a horse's idiosyncrasies. He has to have a feeling for when he should enforce his own style onto the horse and when he has to accept the horse's. In an exceptional partnership, each companion acknowledges the occurrence of good days and bad days. Partners recognize it for what it is and know what they can demand of each other in a given moment. Some days you can have a bit of an argument, on another day you are really in love and everything goes well! As subtle as it may be, you develop a sense for it. You just get to know the mood of your partner and work *around it* on a bad day and *with it* on a good day.

On a good day you might achieve goals you never thought possible. With a special partner you can reach goals you probably only dreamed about. Dutch rider Piet Raymakers said he always knew that he could win a medal one day, that it was only a matter of patience and time to find the right partner. In the mare Ratina Z, he found the perfect partner. They won a team gold and an individual silver at the 1992 Barcelona Olympics.

What is it that makes horses give their rider everything? It can only be a reaction based on mutual trust. Once a horse trusts his partner, he develops and grows; and once a rider has found trust in his horses abilities, he can develop the confidence needed to achieve special accomplishments. If the horse senses that his rider is not the bravest one, he will stop in front of a fence more frequently, but if his rider is daring, it will bring out the horse's courage more freely. Nick Skelton says that he often found himself daring Apollo and that it was then the horse gave his best. In a great partnership one can definitely find similarities between the horse's and the rider's character. With a balance of acceptance and pushing in the right direction, they bring out the best in each other.

This chapter is dedicated to nine great partnerships that have enriched the sport of show jumping and enchanted many fans around the world.

Jos Lansink and Libero

Jos was born in Holland on March 19th 1961. His first introduction to horses came when his father got a Shetland pony for the three children. Jos was only three-years old when he first sat on the pony. He was the only one in the family who 'fell in love with horses' and took riding more seriously, by the age of eight he was competing.

He became Dutch Rural Champion on Surprise, a horse which went on to even greater things with Dutch rider Rob Ehrens. Jos has been based with horse dealer and successful trainer of the Dutch show jumping team, Hans Horn, since 1982. He first made international headlines when he won the small GP of Rotterdam on Felix, back in 1988. Jos and Felix went on to represent their Country at the Seoul Olympics where they came seventh. Jos has been Dutch National Champion of 1990, 1991 and 1992, he won an individual bronze medal at the European Championships in Rotterdam 1989, a team gold and an individual bronze at the 1991 European Championships in La Baule and a team Gold at the 1992 Olympics in Barcelona.

Jos is a very quiet, sympathetic and a most talented rider who seems to be able to adapt effortlessly to all sorts of horses, and also to get their full cooperation and trust in return. He enjoys schooling young horses and only wishes he could find more time to do it. His busy international show jumping schedule doesn't leave much time for training young horses, or for his favourite hobby, watching soccer. But Jos derives a lot of satisfaction from winning big events and admits that his success is partly due to the great understanding he shares with trainer Hans Horn, who also supplies Jos with

the needed horse power. Jos has ridden Libero for four years up to the 1990 World Equestrian Games in Stockholm. Together they have won over 20 classes, including Grands Prix and World Cup qualifiers. In Stockholm the pair placed eleventh.

'I remember that the courses were huge! 1990 started off quite difficult for me because my great partner Felix got sold and normally I would have taken him to Stockholm . . . although Libero had already won some Grands Prix, he was only my second horse then. But Libero went really well there, he stayed clear in the final qualifying event of the Saturday. This was the biggest round he had ever jumped. He gave me a great feeling! Libero is a real fighter, very good mentally and when he kicks out like he sometimes does, this is when he is at his best. I think that stallions do that to play. I like winning too but one has to do it together with the horse, one can't do it alone.'

Nick Skelton and Apollo

Nick was born December 30th 1957 and comes from Warwickshire. He started on ponies, getting his first when he was only three-years old. As a teenager he set his mind on becoming a national hunt jockey, so the winter months were spent watching racing on television for hours. When he paid his first visit to

the Edgar stables with his pony in the summer of 1973, he had no intention of taking up show jumping in a serious way. But Ted Edgar recognised Nick's talent and suggested to Nick's father that he should send his son to train there. So Nick went and stayed for 12 years until he decided at the age of 28, that it was time to move on and set up on his own before it was too late. The years spent at the Edgars were most formative and although Nick was put in at the deep end he always came out on top clocking up a fantastic record of titles.

He started off winning a team silver medal at the Junior European Championships in 1974 which he bettered the following year in taking the Individual Gold at the European Junior Championships. The step into the senior team went smoothly and fortune stayed with him. Nick became a regular member of the triumphant British squad winning European and World Championship medals all along. In 1980 Nick took over the ride of the Dutch-bred gelding Apollo, who had previously been ridden by Geoff Glazzard and formed one of the most outstanding and successful partnerships on the show jumping circuit until Apollo retired at the Hickstead Derby meeting in 1992. The list of major achievements that the pair have won reads as follows: Grand Prix winners at Hickstead twice, Dublin twice, Aachen twice, New York, Toronto, Barcelona, winner of the World Cup qualifier in New York. Winner of the Hickstead Derby twice, Derby of Jerez, winner of numerous Puissance competitions including the Puissance in Dublin twice, Wembley, New York, Toronto. The pair also won a team silver and an individual bronze at the World Championships in Aachen 1986. They went on to win a team gold and an individual bronze at the 1987 European Championships in St Gallen. They won a further team gold at the European Championships in Rotterdam in 1989. Nick describes Apollo as a great all-rounder as the two also won numerous speed classes including the Speed GP in Calgary, and speed competitions during the CSIO in Rome.

Nick's career has not always been as glorious as it sounds. He has had to overcome the shock of sponsors pulling out of the sport as well as the sad deaths of both Airborne and J Nick, who had been two faithful winners for him. But in these moments of darkness, Nick seems to have the incredible ability to always pull back and reach deep down into his soul for strength and optimism. His philosophy is that 'you should never give up in life really. You have to look forward to make the best of what you have.'

Nick is extremely courageous, he demonstrates his fearless love for speed when attacking the fences at high velocity, and is disposed to an acute and ingenious will to win. He simply doesn't know what it means to give up.

When asked about his feeling for Apollo he replied: 'The first things that comes to mind when I think of Apollo is his big heart! He was a real good winner. He could win the fastest speed classes, Puissances, Grand Prix, clock up double clears in Nations Cups. No other horse could have ever done that. He knew a big occasion, and he used to rise to the big arenas like Hickstead, Dublin, Aachen, and Calgary.

'At first I didn't like riding him because he was

so different to what I had ridden before. I used to always have horses where I could control, dominate what was happening. But with Apollo, *he* used to dominate what was happening and in the end I went along with him and learned to ride him! I grew very

fond of him. He was a safe horse because he was very genuine. He was great mentally, when you went to an event and thought that you wanted to win, he very rarely let you down. You had to dare Apollo, the bigger the fences were the better he was. He was sheer braveness together with ability'

John Whitaker and Milton

John Whitaker was born into a farming family in West
Yorkshire August 5th 1955. He is the eldest son of four
children, and together with his younger brother Michael, he
is one of the most accomplished riders in the show jumping
world. He connects with the horses he rides in such a

natural, instinctive and intuitive
manner that one can only conclude
that John was simply born to
become a successful figure in his
chosen sport. John's father Donald
once told me a story that really
sums up John's inborn talent: 'a
neighbouring farmer once brought a
horse to Donald claiming that it was
impossible to ride this horse past a
spooky looking rail without the
horse rearing up, turning round on a
sixpence and bolting off in the
opposite direction! John was only
small then and without telling John
that the horse had a problem,
Donald told his son to sit on the
horse and to ride him past the rail,
out of the yard. John without second thoughts, sat on the
horse and proceeded to take the horse past the rail and out of
the yard. The horse never flinched. The farmer couldn't
believe his eyes! Never before had his horse behaved as well
as that! Donald and the neighbour asked John whether he
had felt any resistance in the horse when approaching the rail
and what he had done to take him past it and out of the yard?

John plainly replied 'no, why I just sat on him. I don't know what I did.' This little anecdote just shows what a calming effect John seems to so effortlessly have on the horses he rides.

A major contributor to British show jumping successes since 1975 when he rode in his first Nations Cup, John became National Champion in 1976 on his wonderfully eccentric partner Ryan's Son. The two went on to clinch, amongst other wins, a team as well as an individual silver medal in Rotterdam 1980 at the substitute games (All the top nations boycotted the Moscow Olympics). John and Ryan's Son won a further team silver medal at the Los Angeles games in 1984.

A year later another super star this time in the form of Milton made it to John's yard. The two have won numerous titles including seven World Cup Qualifiers, two Volvo World Cup Finals, team gold and individual silver at the European Championships of 1987 in St Gallen, a team and individual gold at the European Championships in Rotterdam in 1989, a team bronze and an individual silver at the World Equestrian Games of 1990 in Stockholm, and a team silver at the 1991 European Championships in La Baule. Milton is the only horse to date that has won over £1000,000 in his career.

When asked about his feelings on winning two gold medals in Rotterdam with Milton, John replied in his quiet, humorous way: 'I was in the lead and Michael was last to go. I knew if he had a fence down, I had won. I didn't really want him to have a fence down . . . but I wanted to win. A funny feeling that! The main thing was that we would finish first and second. A few years ago in Dinard we also lay first and second before the last day, but then we both lost . . . so we said as long as we stayed first and second, it didn't really matter who was going to win.

'To have a horse like Milton, just makes my job much easier. He is such a pleasure to ride! He loves the job and it makes life so much easier when he is wanting to do it. He is at his best when he is fresh and the fitter he is the better he jumps, so I try and keep him like that. I try and save him for the best shows, the best classes and keep him happy and fresh in his mind. I see how he feels and should he get tired, I would miss a few shows. Milton is 16 now, a horse is at his best between 11 and 13 but to be honest, he doesn't really feel any different, and on his day he still feels as good as ever.

'Barcelona might have come a bit too late for him. The first three horses were all young between eight and ten. I made a mistake on the final course, underestimated the size, I was a bit off, but four or five years ago, he would have probably jumped it.

I remember the first ever jump I did with him, I knew that he was better than average, I didn't know how good but the way he left the floor, you could feel the power! He is a horse that gives you more determination because you feel how much he loves the atmosphere of, say Gothenburg, where the public love him so much. He gives you more confidence. You know that the public is behind you and that Milton is trying. All this gives you more incentive. I feel that it is a privilege to have been able to ride him.'

Ludger Beerbaum and Classic Touch

The Olympic Champion from Barcelona 1992 Ludger Beerbaum was born August 26th 1963. Compared to his rivals, he started to ride relatively late in life. He was only 11 and believe it or not, he started on a donkey! No wonder that Ludger has the reputation of being able to get anything to jump. Discovered by former national trainer Herman Schridde, his career simply rocketed. He won various German junior as well as European young rider titles on his way to a place in the senior team. From 1985 to 1989 Ludger rode for the Paul Schockemöhle stable. In 1988 he became National Champion on Landlord, the horse which he was due to ride at the Olympics in Seoul. Landlord went lame just a day before the contest was scheduled to start and Ludger had to resort to his team mate Dirk Hafemeister's reserve horse The Freak.

Ludger, who had only sat on The Freak for the first time the day before, accomplished a first-round score of only one quarter of a fault for exceeding the time allowed. The second time round he was very unlucky to have clipped the last fence on Olaf Petersen's Olympic course to reach the finish with four faults and a total of four and a quarter out of the two rounds. A result that only Olympic Champion of Los Angeles 1984, Joe Fargis was to match. Ludger, in his modesty explained, wearing the Olympic team gold medal round his neck, that: 'It wasn't really such an achievement, after all the horse had been ridden by other riders before and had always gone

well.' But the charismatic German couldn't hide his excellence for too long.

In spite of leaving the powerful Schockemöhle stable and setting off on his own in the south of Germany, sponsored by the meat merchant Alexander Moxel, Ludger's potential and dexterity were still unchartered. Well-known for his strong nerves and his determination he won a team silver medal at the 1990 World Equestrian Games in Stockholm on the German bred mare Gazelle. Although Ludger is as adept and efficient on a gelding, a mare or a stallion, he definitely has a unique touch when riding mares. He immediately struck a congenial partnership

with his Olympic mount from Barcelona, the Holsteiner mare Classic Touch.

Ludger and the mare had been together a little over a year, when the then seven-year old mare won her first GP at the Horse of the Year Show in October 1991. Classic Touch helped Ludger to win his second National Title in 1992 as well as being part of the victorious German team in Aachen before travelling

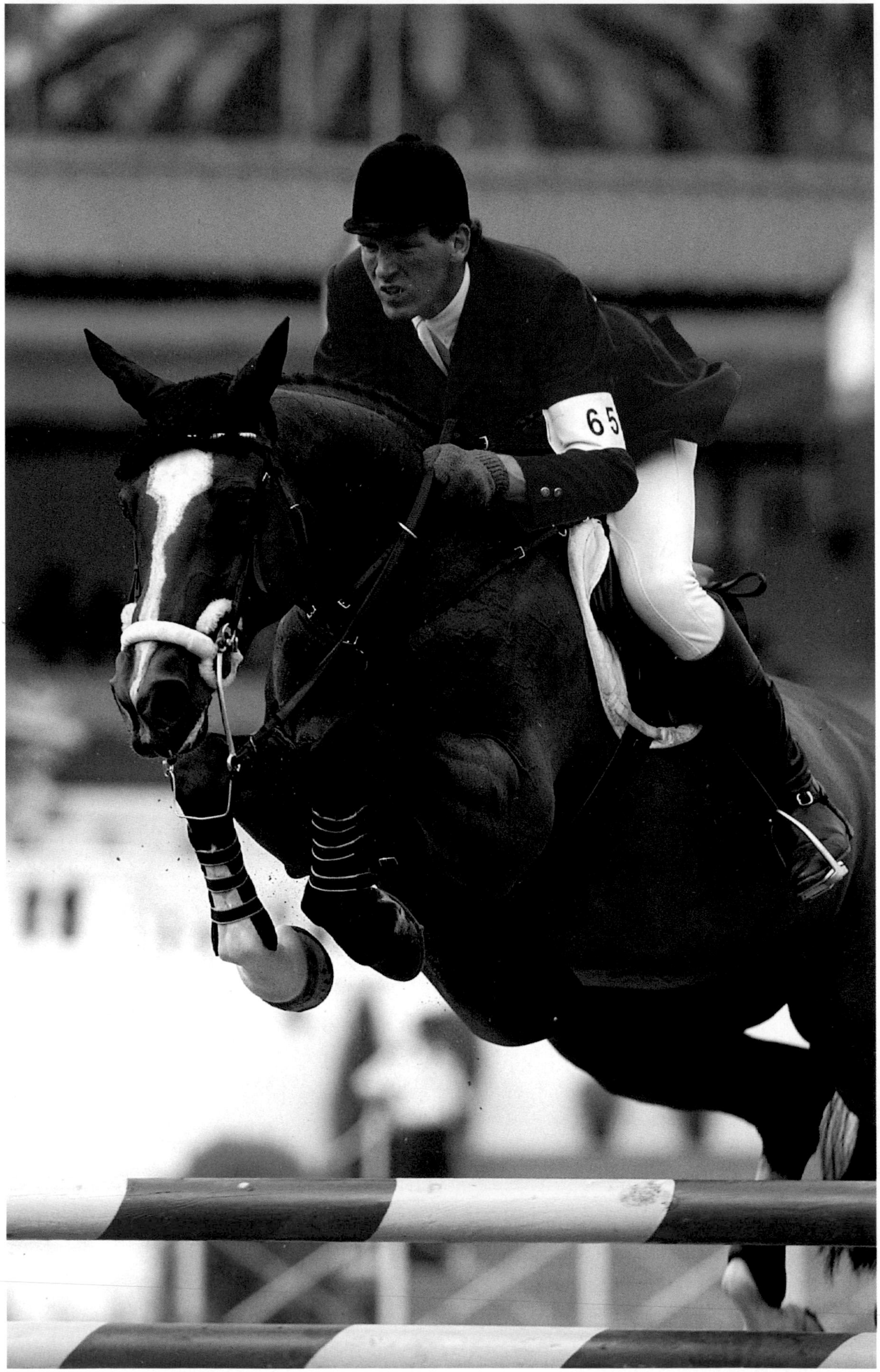
65

to Barcelona. At the Olympics, Ludger had to reach deep down into his mental resources like never before. After jumping a faultless first round in the team event, disaster struck in the second round when the mare's hackamore broke, and Ludger was left with no control over Classic Touch. The only option he had left, was to throw himself to the ground to save his neck. The chances of qualifying for the individual final seemed so distant now and all Ludger's hopes lay in achieving a good result over the third course. Coolness, accurate riding and total understanding between Classic Touch and Ludger gave hope to the objective. The duo qualified for the final and wrote history in achieving the only double clear over the somewhat controversial Olympic courses.

'The nicest feeling of my entire life! The biggest success! These are the feelings I get by looking at this picture. I think that this feeling is going to stay with me forever. Never before had I ridden a horse of Classic Touch's quality. I don't want to compare her to Milton because he is the horse of the century and one couldn't compare any horse to him, but I think that apart from Milton, there is no better horse in the world than Classic Touch. She is untouchable!

She has a sensational character. I believe that she was born to be a jumper. She is very keen every day — even a little too keen. One has to contain her because of her enthusiasm, she attacks her job with great intensity. I decided to ride her in a hackamore from the start when she was seven so that I could

throttle her eagerness without having to pull too hard. In a bit she only pushes against it and I don't get through... She has such a generous personality. Even when one has to compete in the rain, she surpasses herself.'

Michael Whitaker and Monsanta

The first thing that springs to mind when one hears the name Michael Whitaker, is that he is John's younger brother. But, Michael born on March 17th 1960 has a record of accomplishments that leaves his rivals and show jumping fans around the globe in an equal state of amazement. Right from his days as a successful junior — he won a team bronze in 1976 and a team gold in 1978 — Michael was destined to become a star in his own right. His aggressive and yet controlled style, captures the audience and brings excitement to the sport. He proves his incredible versatility over and over by winning all sorts of classes on a number of different mounts. He seems to be able to adapt to a variety of horses in no time at all. He can sit quiet like he had to when competing on his great winner Warren Point and he can animate any horse in the likes of Monsanta, who is a little 'stuffy' as Michael describes him.

Modestly he states that there is 'No secret to my riding, I have been doing it from when I was so young, I just get on a horse and try to adapt to it.' When asked what horse he prefers, he answered with a big smile: 'I prefer a horse that is right in the middle of Warren Point and Monsanta, not too hot and not too cold!' Part of Michael's charm is definitely his spontaneity and his natural approach to it all. His sense of humour surfaces in the most unpredictable situations. When riding Gogshall Spot On during a speed class in Gothenburg 1988 and the angle Michael had chosen for Gogshall resulted in the little spotted gelding's refusal, Michael reacted

spontaneously by picking a Daffodil out of the flower arrangement and pretending it was his whip, gave the horse a smack and finished the course.

Michael is extremely keen and has a great desire to win. He is emotional and gets far more upset when things go slightly wrong than John does. One can always detect a true feeling of disappointment in Michael's behaviour when he has had a fence down,

especially when riding for the team. 'It is harder to ride in the team because you don't want to let any of the others down.' He had to overcome his greatest disappointment to date during the Olympics of Los Angeles when a refusal by Amanda at the treble combination meant that he lost all chances of an individual medal that had seemed within reach.

Like all true sportsmen, however, he is a real fighter and his partner Monsanta, gives Michael his entire support and devotion. The two first joined forces in 1989 shortly before the European Championships when Sir Phil Harris decided to buy the Irish gelding for Michael, since he was definitely lacking in horsepower. Monsanta had already served his former rider the talented Gillian Greenwood very well. So he was used to big fences, and Michael adjusted marvellously to his new partner. They won a team gold, and an individual silver medal at the European Championship in Rotterdam, 1989 as well as clinching the world's biggest prize-money by winning the Calgary Grand Prix — all within a month. Their success continued. Michael and Monsanta won the Hickstead Derby in 1991 as well as 1992.

'Monsanta is a real genuine horse, he tries his heart out all the time. He doesn't have Milton's scope but then again not many do. He loves the big arenas like Hickstead, Aachen, Calgary. Monsanta's wins at both Derbies were unbelievable, especially the second one because the weather conditions were very bad and Monsanta had just come from the Olympics. This just showed what a great character he has.'

Tina Cassan and Genesis

Berkshire Girl Tina Cassan was very nearly born on a Pony on June 12th 1965. Her family has always been involved with horses and Tina was put on her first pony at the age of two. She joined the Pony Club and competed in all disciplines, gathering experience while gradually making it through the ranks into Juniors, Young Riders and finally Seniors. While riding with Hampshire-based horse dealer Freddie Welch Tina first started to make a name for herself. She rode in her first Senior Nations Cup in Prague 1989, where she scored the only double clear round of the competition. She has an inborn hunger to win and admits that at times she would even be 'a little too hungry'. She is extremely ambitious, and has all the coolness and single mindedness necessary to be a top rider. Moving to Yorkshire in 1990, where she rode for Fred Brown, her partnership with the Hanovarian bred Genesis started. It wasn't an obvious one right from the start. Tina was really challenged to show her skills in trying to train him: 'He was dreadful and very

difficult to ride at first. He ran round the corners, stuck his nose up in the air, couldn't change legs, but I played around with him, and learned how to ride and love him.' Before too long the partnership grew together. In 1990 they had won the Championships for six-year olds, at Hickstead, two Olympic Star Spotters Qualifiers, as well as the Final of the Olympic Star Spotters at the Horse of the Year Show. In 1991 they won a few AIT classes at home, and went on to score some remarkable results abroad. They were members of the winning Nations Cup team in Drammen and Washington, they came second in the Grand Prix in New York, and won the World Cup Qualifier as well as the Masters in Toronto, which Tina rates as Genesis' greatest achievement to date because 'the fences were really huge and we beat Ian Miller on Big Ben.'

In the Spring of 1992 the duo travelled to Del Mar for the Volvo World Cup Final, a show that neither Tina nor the show jumping fraternity will ever forget. The Californian incident had, to say the least, really tested Tina's coolness. She showed real strength of character when she kept her nerves while

controversy raged over the timing at
the start of the first leg in the Volvo
World Cup Final. Before she had even
started her round of the table A
competition, the clock was already
showing over 30 seconds. The tricky
thing was that the judges had already
rung the bell which means that the
rider has to start his/her round within a
minute or else they risk elimination.
Tina was determined not to leave the
arena before things were sorted out.
She rates her experience there as
unbelievable: 'I was mad, raging and
screaming at the judges to put the
timing back to zero before I would start
but they wouldn't.' It took 15 to 20
minutes before the judges agreed to
give Tina a fresh start. All of that time
Tina and Genesis (then only eight) had
to stay in the arena and wait. 'Genesis
was unbelievable to put up with all of
that. The entire crowd got up on their
feet. It was like in a football stadium. I
had never seen anything like it before.
The time we had to wait felt like a life
time. All I could think of was Oh my
God, we came all this way and now I
am going to be gonged out on the first
day. Genesis was fresh, wild and felt
fantastic, he was just going sky-high in
the warm-up class the day before.'

When the judges finally gave the go ahead after having watched the incident on video, the pair really showed what they were made of and cleared all of the fences. From that moment on the crowd was very firmly behind Tina and cheered for her every time she came into the ring. The pair placed seventh overall.

Genesis, as well as Tina, seems to rise to the occasion. Later that year, they were members of the winning team in the Hickstead Nations Cup where Tina got psyched up to do well primarily because Hickstead is her favourite show ground, but also because Team *Chef* Ronnie Massarella had told his team that they were probably not strong enough to win in front of the home crowd.

'I am very stubborn, so Ronnie's pessimism helped me because when people tell me that I cannot do something, or that it is too difficult for me, I am determined to prove them wrong.'

Tina, very competitive, always strives for perfection. 'Even if I win a class and I feel I haven't ridden to the best of my ability or that I feel that I have done something wrong, I chew over it the whole time'. She thinks that although part of being a perfectionist is inborn, it also has a lot to do with Freddie Welch's training: 'I remember having won a Young Riders Qualifier and being really delighted with the horse and pleased with myself. When I walked up to Freddie thinking that he would say fantastic, which he very rarely said anyway, he only said "You stupid cow, you just burned out your horse. You won by seven seconds when you should

have only won by one or two seconds."' Tina knows that Freddie had a good point and felt disappointed in herself when she won the Queen Elizabeth Cup on Genesis by a margin of over seven seconds.

It is more important for Tina to win titles than GP classes. One of her greatest ambitions is to ride at the Olympics in Atlanta but the sudden death of Fred Brown in January 1993 sadly resulted in Tina loosing all of his horses which puts her future plans on hold for the time being. Genesis was sold to American rider George Lindemann Jr.

'I have always dreamed of winning the Queen Elizabeth Cup. Winning it this year came as a real relief because the field of competitors wasn't as strong as it has been in previous years and I would have never forgiven myself had I not won it. Genesis was unbelievable. After the CSIO meeting at Hickstead the selectors made us go to Kapellen where Genesis just wasn't himself. We had his blood tested and he had to rest. I didn't ride again before coming back from Kapellen, until five minutes before the class. He was great and tried his heart out.

'Genesis is a difficult and cocky horse. If you ever try to cross him, he will fight you until he drops dead. He has a mind of his own but he is very lovable. The more difficult and the more fighting he is, the better he jumps. I love him more than any other horse, not because he was the most successful for me but because he is such a lovely character, he would always neigh at you when you came out of the house. The greatest thing about riding Genesis was that I always knew I had all the power in the world.'

Marie Edgar and Surething

Without doubt Marie Edgar has one of the most enviable pedigrees a show jumper can possibly have. She was born on February 28th 1971, to father Ted Edgar and mother Liz Edgar—née Broome. Ted is a successful horseman and an accomplished trainer. He has produced top riders in the likes of Nick Skelton, Geoff Luckett, Leslie McNaught-Maendli. Liz Edgar is one of the best women riders England has seen to date. She won the Queen Elizabeth II Cup a record five times and is the first woman rider to have won the GP of Aachen in 1980 on Forever. She has also been the member of the winning British team on five occasions.

Marie was given her first pony by her grandfather Fred Broome at the age of two and a half. She then moved rapidly through ponies and started to ride horses at the age of 12. She found horses much easier mainly because she admits to not being the bravest of riders and that is why 'Dad put me on horses quite early because there was always somebody around to help and even get on the horses to sort them out when it was necessary.'

Surething appeared when Marie was 15 and she admits that she couldn't ride him at first. 'Geoff Luckett rode him in novice classes and then mother rode him before I got him back.' In 1988, when Marie was only 17, the pair proved that they found each other by winning the Grand Prix at Royal Windsor. Marie recalls that Surething had almost been sold to Switzerland, but 'after we won, it was

the end of the sale! Dad didn't dare sell him.' A good thing too, because the same year Marie and Surething won an individual gold and a team silver medal at the Junior European Championships, the Young Rider of the Year and the National 21 Championship! The following year the pair repeated their success of becoming Junior European Individual Champions and went one better with the team making it two gold medals at the Championships, their last year as juniors.

Moving up to young riders, the partnership stayed just as consistent. In 1990 they won a team and an individual European Gold medal. At the 1991 Young Riders European Championships Marie stayed just as successful this time claiming both titles with Rapier. At the European Young Riders Championships of the following year Marie was back to riding Surething to a Team Gold and an Individual Bronze medal. 'Surething had been very unlucky that year. The morning of the individual event, he got bitten on his leg by a fly which resulted in a big front leg . . . but he gave his best and we still got the Bronze.'

Regardless of all her titles, Marie has both feet planted quite firmly on the ground. When asked what she thought her strongest point was, she replied with a big smile: 'Having been a Junior and a Young rider. As yet what really made me win all of these titles was having had Surething, with him I was just slightly over horsed!' Her father believes that 'it is all in the genes,' and her mother adds very quickly to his remark that it is 'like with race horses, they have always had a good mother!' On a more serious note the whole family agrees that it is mostly down to opportunity. 'You can start off with a talent but if you don't have the opportunity you get nowhere.'

Although Marie considers the transition from young riders to seniors a big step, she is very determined to do well and certainly shows the right

amount of will to win. Her main ambition is to win the Queen Elizabeth II Cup and take on the best riders in the world. 'Not necessarily beating them straight away but holding your own in the same classes as them. I'd like to be the best I can be.' She enjoys competing abroad and is getting used to riding at the top senior level. When riding in Zurich in

March 1993, she very nearly won the main class. Leading by two seconds in the jump off, Surething lost his footing and the two fell. Marie reflected on it with humour calling it 'My big impact into International Show Jumping. I would have won £35,000 and I did a somersault instead.'

'To begin with Surething was difficult to ride because he had such a long stride and he struggled to adjust. You always had to be on the right stride. He could never slow up at the end. We have gained more confidence in each other now, and he has become a much easier horse to ride. He is so fast and very careful. If you get to the fence in the right place, he will try his heart out. He likes crowds, the atmosphere really gets him going. He can get very naughty when waiting in the tunnel. He will have a bit of a rear and leap around. Surething is my friend, a winner with a heart of gold. Everything he has done, he has always done to please.'

Ian Millar and Big Ben

Ian Millar is the most popular and most successful rider that Canada has seen to date. Starting with the 1972 Olympics from Munich, he has competed at five consecutive Olympic Games, at the alternative Games held in Rotterdam 1980, as well as representing Canada at four consecutive Pam American Games. He rode at three World Championships, and 12 Volvo World Cup Finals. His greatest achievements include winning a team gold in 1980, a team silver and an individual bronze at the Pam Am Games the year before, a team silver at the Pam Am Games in 1983, and a team as well as an individual gold at the Pam Am Games in 1987. Indoors he was twice the winner of the Volvo World Cup Final in 1988 (Gothenburg) and 1989 (Tampa).

Born on January 6th 1947, he started to ride at the age of ten. Ian's father was in the army and was posted from eastern Canada out west to Edmonton Alberta. Ian remembers that in his mind he figured that going west meant horses, cowboys and indians! In order to keep their son quiet, Ian's parents finally gave in to his demands, and the whole family including Ian's sisters started to take riding lessons. They all stayed very interested in horses, particularly his mother who always kept horses at home. Ian rode western as well as English, competing in all the western gymkhanas such as pole bending and barrel racing. By riding in both styles, Ian felt that his first few years were well rounded. Because jumping looked the most exciting, fun and challenging, it became his real interest right from the start and it was when moving back east at 15 that show jumping became his real passion. Ian got very involved with the Pony Club competing in one, two and three day events, and recalls finding it most enjoyable. 'In another life I could have easily been an eventer.'

Although Ian was dead keen on horses, he went on to study business administration and had careers as a stockbroker and radio broadcaster before devoting his entire life to horses. What remains from these days, is the very mental, analytical and convincing approach that Ian brings to his riding. 'I am a persevering son of a gun. Once I start in a certain direction and I figure that the plan is right and the idea correct, I will just repeat and repeat. This is how I train horses. This is basically how I train myself.

'Like most top riders Ian has learned to be philosophical in his analysis. 'With horses, if a problem is large enough, it is obvious, but there are so many little subtle things about horses physically as well as mentally that only become apparent when they are put under stress. When you go to a big show, you might think that you have everything under control, yet you can watch how many amazing surprises can happen. Often you'll come back from a competition and you'll never know why it didn't

work out . . . the next time you'd ride the same, you'd put a leg on each side, a rein in each hand, and the horse's head between the standards and you'd win! The best riders as well as the best horses are forever students.'

Ian feels quite comfortable looking at life through his horse's eyes. 'It means scaling things down and simplifying them, being careful about the way one communicates stress to a horse because there is positive stress and negative stress. The minute I get on a horse, we are working together. We are partners.' One of his greatest partners is the Belgium bred 17.3hh hands Big Ben. Ian got him as a seven-year old through Dutch rider and horse dealer Emile Hendrix in the Autumn of 1987. 'At the beginning I had my doubts whether Big Ben's character would allow him to be trained. He was so strong minded!'

With Ian's tactics of perseverance and repetition,

the two soon developed a unique bond, coupled with tremendous understanding for one another. There is no other horse in the world that would come back from two severe colic operations and a major travelling accident and still produce winning performances for his master. The first show after his trailer accident, Big Ben won three out of three classes at the Spruce Meadows spring meeting. Ian considers winning the 1989 World Cup Final in Tampa Big Ben's greatest achievement. 'It was remarkable because he won outright, winning all three legs.'

Winning the Du Maurier Grand Prix twice also means a lot to 'Mr. Canada', as he is nicknamed in his own country.

'It is really a big deal to win the Du Maurier. To win it is great for me, great for Big Ben's owners, for the sponsors and the people of Canada. Winning in Spruce Meadows is truly one of the best feelings one can have. 1991 was so special. The crowd was electric. The more they responded, the louder they cheered, the higher he jumped! The fabulous thing about Big Ben is his combination of desire, courage and his mental characteristics. He is so smart. The best compliment one can give an athlete is to say that he is efficient. Big Ben is extremely efficient. He does what he has to do. He doesn't waste a lot of power, energy, or moves. He focuses and does it. If he was a person he would be one of those strong willed, strong charactered, positive, focused, workaholic, high energy type of individuals. He has won just as much when conditions haven't suited him

— not even a little bit. He just grows above them. 'Our partnership started off with a mutual respect for certain physical and mental qualities then it developed into a working relationship with pretty big admiration for one another and the beginning of a friendship. From that it grew into a whole working relationship where we would both know each other's moves before we knew them ourselves.

'I really like his character. If he was a person now, he'd be my best friend.'

Eric Navet and Quito de Baussy

French, World and European Champion Eric Navet is one of the most natural, passionate and sympathetic horseman on the international show jumping circuit. Born on May 9th 1959 to ex-international show jumper and horse breeder Alain Navet, Eric never questioned whether he was interested in horses or not. The fascination he developed came through his own pedigree: 'It was very simple for me, it all came so naturally, and I feel that I have an advantage over children who where not born into it like myself. I feel that it was much easier for me because we always had a lot of horses at home.'

Eric got his first pony at the age of four. At seven he used to travel every weekend together with his father and top horses to compete in what he describes as 'little show numbers at national shows, where a small course was put up for ponies to entertain the public before the start of the Grand Prix.' At 12, which was the minimum age for official shows, Eric started to compete on young horses. He very quickly moved on to Juniors and rode at three European Junior Championships, winning an individual and team silver medal in 1976 and an individual gold and a team silver medal in 1977. He achieved his first big success on a mare called Doris, which had previously been ridden by Nelson Pessoa, winning a big Derby in front of Hervé Godignon on Electre, the duo that everybody had set out to beat at the time. In his early days as a senior, Eric was often seen as the fifth rider at CSIO meetings because, although he didn't really dispose of top horses, team *chefs* had always thought a lot of his talent.

Like both his grandfather and father, Eric has a big passion for breeding. 'I am very interested in breeding because I have always had young horses to ride and I love training young horses.' He considers his interest a necessity for his profession: 'if you want to benefit from having good horses to bring on, you have to try and breed them. 'My idea is to always have a rota of young horses to bring on so that one is never short of quality six-, seven- and eight-year olds who have also gained experience from competing with me as four-year olds.' The right selection from generation to generation is very important to the Navet family. They always keep their best performing mares and best stallions for breeding. Eric doesn't believe in quantity breeding, it is the quality that fascinates him. It is for this reason that Eric has kept the mare Nai-Ka, a puissance specialist and Quito de Baussy. 'I am already really looking forward to having the first foal out of Nai-Ka and

Quito to work with!' Eric is dedicated to riding the youngsters and expresses a genuine longing to ride the four-year olds at their first shows again. 'I'm really taken by the four-year olds, and I'm starting to ride them again because it has been three years. I really miss it.'

Eric believes that it was a combination of his father's help, together with riding young horses that developed his skills as a rider. He puts the success he has achieved with Quito de Baussy down to a partnership that started when Quito was very young. 'Why Quito gives me such satisfaction is truly because I have done everything with him. I broke him in, I schooled him and I took him to his first show. I did it all from A to Z.'

Eric is a highly motivated competitor, and derives immense satisfaction from being able to measure himself with the elite of riders; and by bringing his own young horses up to international standard. He has the gift of not letting ambition get in the way of choosing and preparing his horses. He is very cautious and sensible in judging about when and how far he can push a horse. 'At seven horses are in a year of mental transition. It is a difficult year because one could be tempted to overface them. Horses have a big heart at that age because they haven't been asked to give too much. Their heart is fresh, unspoiled and they are ready and willing to do everything one asks of them. One has seen exceptional horses as seven year olds because they have given everything and then they were finished.' Eric had taken it very slowly with Quito de Baussy. He had only jumped him in 1.30m classes never pushing him against the clock. It was only toward to end of his season as a seven-year old that he decided after long deliberation to take Quito to a CSI in Fontainebleau and put him in a derby. 'When I walked the course, I thought this is crazy, too high and I began to have my doubts. I started to regret having entered him. I decided to take him but to only jump the first three or four fences before I would retire him, but he jumped so well that I carried on. He stayed clear and placed third.' Up to then Eric had never really thought of Quito as an exceptional horse, rather as 'A horse amongst many I had to ride' and he believes that 'One had to put the fences up for Quito to tell me "but of course I can jump these heights!"'

From that moment on the pair went from strength to strength, they placed second in the Grand Prix of Grenoble and started their CSIO career early in 1990 at Lucerne, where they won the Grand Prix with three clear rounds as well as

clocking up a double clear round in the Nations Cup. Eric remembers how the press praised the horse and how they all predicted that he would be a sure bet for the World Equestrian Games later in the year. 'I told them no, that I was not interested.' Now that he knew what a superstar Quito was, he didn't want to risk him. 'I felt that he was too young and inexperienced for the Championships. I didn't want to break my toy.'

Three months later, however, things were different: team-mate and Olympic Champion Pierre Durand convinced Eric that he wouldn't be risking anything by taking Quito to the World Equestrian Games. He persuaded Eric that he was capable of solving all the technical problems the pair would encounter, and that Quito was so well schooled that he would respond well therefore not run into heartbreaking difficulties. Motivated by all of this, Eric called team chef Patrick Caron and said: 'Two months ago I told you that I didn't want to go to the World Equestrian Games. Now, I am not saying that I want to go, but should you need me, I'd go there.'

Shortly after that conversation, Hervé Godignon's mare La Belletière injured herself and Patrick Caron called Eric telling him that he was needed.

Judging by Eric's career, his character consists of a well-balanced combination of thoughtfulness, gentleness, ambition and a love of adventure. His ambitions are to acquire an Olympic Individual Gold medal to hang next to his World and European ones, and to win the Volvo World Cup title. That will

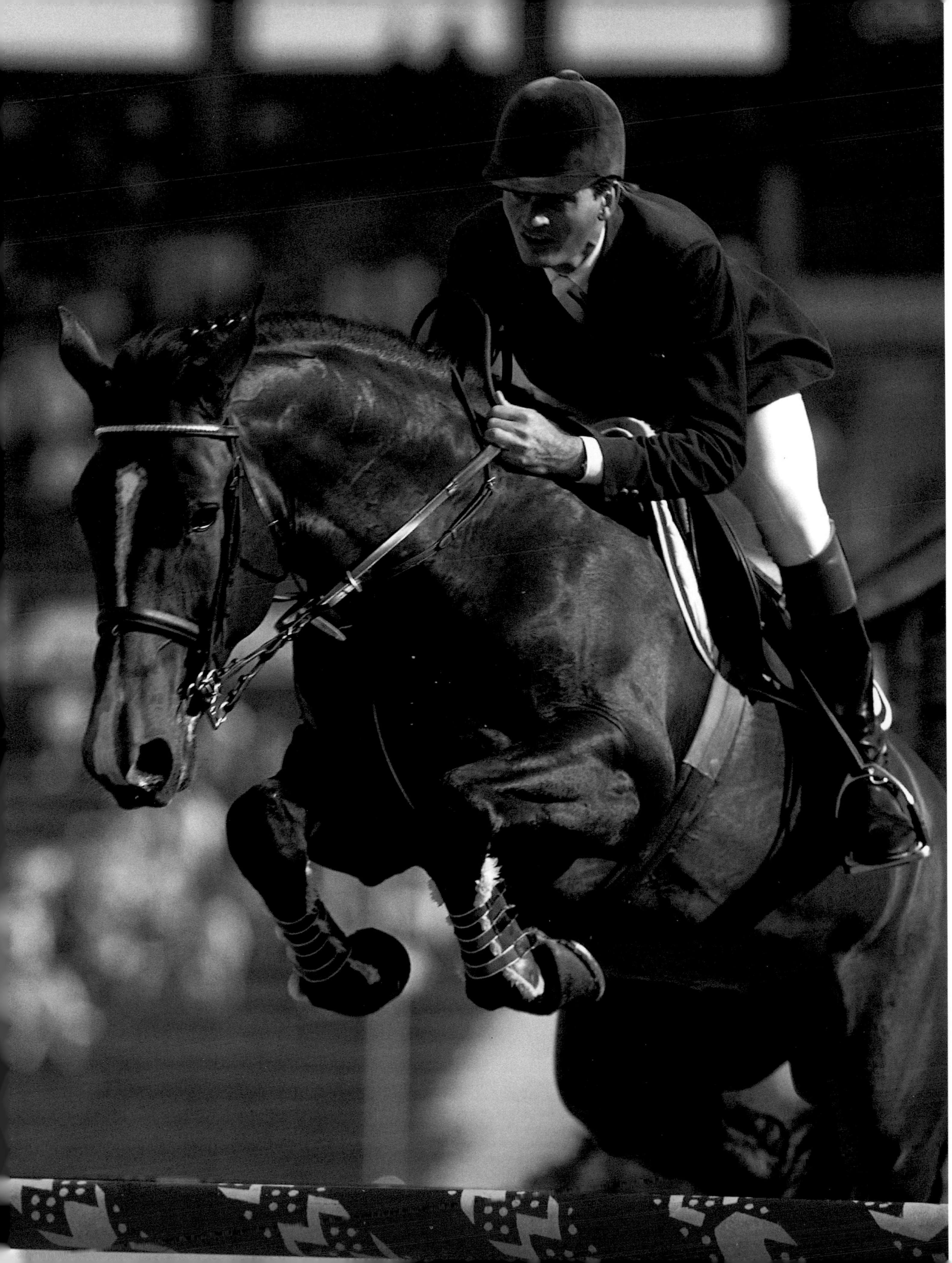

keep him occupied for several years. One thing he has always stressed however, was that his main objective is to have the longest possible career at the top level rather than collecting titles. 'Of course I felt fantastic winning in Stockholm, but the first thing that crossed my mind was that the worst thing that could happen to me was for it to end here, in which case I would have preferred never to have won the title of World Champion.' His fears were understandable because they are the fears of every dedicated person. A year later however, the partnership proved their quality yet again by winning the title of European Champion in La Baule.

'Quito's principal quality is his head. He is a horse with an exceptional temperament. He always wants to please. He never questions himself, never doubts. He has unprecedented trust in me. We have been allies for a long time. His trust in me has been built up from the days I broke him in. Quito also has weak points, as all horses do. His jumping technique is not perfect, but his deficiency is compensated for by his excellent mental qualities. Unlike the initial doubts I had about Quito's greatness, my father had every faith in Quito — a bit of a 'breeders feeling' in conjunction with recognizing a good jump in a horse. First of all Quito is Jalisco's son and Jalisco has proven himself more than once, but more interestingly, my father won the Grand Prix of Amsterdam and Brussels on a mare called Luma. Luma had a full sister called Jolieta who produced Quito's mother. So it is not such a stroke of luck after all. Quito is really the baby of the family.'

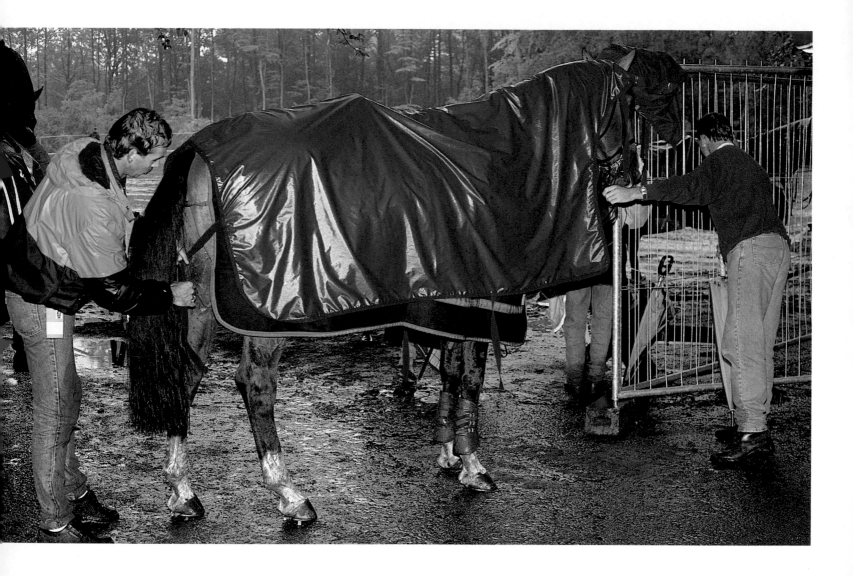

BEHIND
THE SCENES

Grooms are a special breed of people. Being a travelling groom to a top international rider necessitates a unique way of life: one that is both hard and rewarding. Grooms get to travel the world but in conditions far removed from tourist luxury. They usually live in the horsebox while travelling or at the show itself. Very rarely do they get a hotel room for the shows. Perks are few and far between but sometimes show organisers will give them spending money or coupons for food. From the outset, a groom carries enormous responsibility: he or she is left in charge of very valuable, top show horses, and is often seen driving the lorry from one country to another. Riders very often must fly home to attend to business before flying back to the next location. The groom must be one hundred percent trustworthy. They are a special link in the complex chain that makes or breaks a successful, winning combination.

Being with the horses for most of the time, grooms get to understand their behaviour and character almost totally. So the groom becomes a vital source of knowledge to the rider. They will be the first to spot any changes to the horse's physical or mental disposition and will relate that to the rider. Once grooms have found a person they like working for, they will stay with them for a long time. They give every necessary support, not only by turning the horses out immaculately for the ring, but also by helping in the warm up for a class. Last minute preparations in the collecting ring are as important as the work that goes into training a horse at home. By putting fences up and watching the horses carefully, they can give reassurance and confidence.

They practically work all year round. During the outdoor season they work come rain or sun. During the winter months when the circuit moves indoors, working hours will be very long but in general the grooms prefer it to struggling with muddy and wet conditions. The life demands a lot of self sacrifice; their entire day revolves around the horse. From getting up at the crack of dawn to feed the horses, to putting them to bed at night after a demanding competition, it is no exaggeration to say that it is a labour of love. Each grooms brings his or her own special skill and personality to the job, yet they have certain characteristics in common. They usually range between the age of 22 to 30. Most of them are shy about revealing their age and believe that they look and certainly feel much older than they really are! Some come from horse-minded families, others have watched show jumping on television and fallen in love with the idea of looking after a winning horse and working for a top rider.

THE CSIO ROTTERDAM IS TRADITIONALLY HELD IN AUGUST AND IT USUALLY RAINS AT LEAST ON ONE OF THE DAYS IF NOT THE WHOLE WEEK!
HERE GROOMS DESPERATELY TRY TO KEEP THE HORSE AND TACK AS DRY AS POSSIBLE. ONE THING THEY GET USED TO RIGHT FROM THE START IS TO ATTEND TO THE HORSE'S NEEDS BEFORE THINKING ABOUT THEMSELVES

A good win or helping a sick horse to get better makes all the hard work worthwhile. Nothing is more rewarding for a groom than being part of a successful team. Success doesn't always mean winning a major championship, it could mean being instrumental in sorting out a horse's problem. It is the achievements and improvements that matter most.

Although some grooms express the need to work

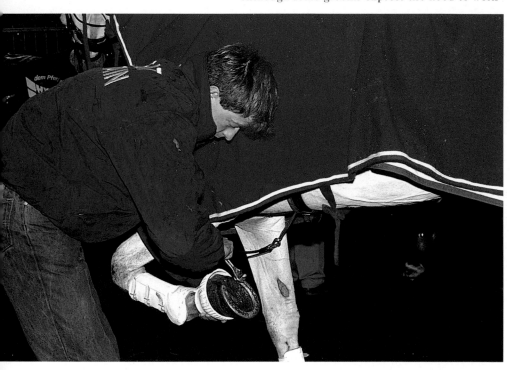

MARK BEEVER, AT THE 1991 CSIO
ROTTERDAM IS SCREWING THE
STUDS INTO FIORELLA'S SHOE.
CHOOSING THE RIGHT STUDS FOR
AN EVENT IS IMPORTANT. FOR
THEY GIVE THE HORSE THE
NECESSARY GRIP AND
CONFIDENCE TO TACKLE THE
FENCES

for a champion, their lives are not always blessed with the glory of a win. They often witness drama and defeat too. Sometimes they get blamed for an unfortunate mishap in the ring. Often they are the first person a rider will share his or her thoughts with once they come out of the ring. And very often they are the most interested party to tell!

Mark Beever has been travelling groom to international rider Nick Skelton for the past seven years. Before joining the Skelton team, he worked for ex-international rider Sally Mapleson. He doesn't come from a horse-minded family, nonetheless he got hooked on horses at the age of ten. Here are some of his reflections on his work.

'At shows, hours are really long especially during the winter season. You don't have a routine as such because it depends on when the classes are. You have to juggle around with your duties. The most important thing is to get up, feed, muck out, walk the horses out before Nick comes. Then I have breakfast *sometime* in the morning . . . at shows you soon learn that you have to be really flexible. Feeding is important: horses must get fed three hours before the class, then you get them ready.

'I like staying at home, I have travelled to shows for too long. I still like the shows but you can't go on doing them forever. It is always in the back of your mind how long you should go on. For me, winning at the shows makes the job worthwhile. I also get some financial reward when Nick wins. I couldn't work for a rider that didn't win. I have got to work for the best!'

Caroline Hancock has been a groom ever since she left school at the age of 16. She has been travelling groom to Swiss rider Lesley Mc Naught-Maendli for the past seven years. She doesn't come from a horse minded-family but as far as she can remember she always wanted to have a pony. At the age of 12 she finally got one. For her becoming a groom was an obvious choice.

'It has to be for the love of horses. It is

exhilarating to be around them. It doesn't always have to be winning. It's rewarding when you have a sick horse that gets better, or if a horse has a problem with something and it gets better, it mends and starts work again. When this happens, you have achieved something. Achievements and improvements are very satisfying to me.

'You have to enjoy it to do it! If you are not enjoying it you are not going to be good at it. It involves so much — too much! If you are not happy to put in the time, there is no point in doing it. If you enjoy doing something, then it is not difficult and it comes easy. I prefer travelling to staying at home. Maybe because of all the hard work you have put in at home. You get to be there and see the results. When you are present at the shows it is the real thing

GIVING THE HORSES A WALK OUT IN THE MORNING BEFORE A LONG DAY OF COMPETITION GETS THEM STARTED OFF ON A GOOD NOTE. NOT ONLY DO THE HORSES GET A CHANCE TO STRETCH THEIR LEGS, IT IS ALSO OCCUPIES THEIR MINDS as opposed to sitting at home, hoping to get news.

'Being a groom means being there most of the time. It means being around, noticing the small things that if you didn't know the horse you wouldn't notice. If you don't notice the little things then it could develop into a big problem . . . you think, eat, drink, sleep, walk, dream horses. I do anyway! If I have a problem with a horse and I might be going out for dinner, talking with friends, I would still be thinking about how to put the problem right. It is one hundred percent devotion.

GROOM TO BRITISH RIDER
MICHAEL WHITAKER, LINDSEY
BREWERTON ENJOYS A BIT OF
SUNSHINE WHILE CLEANING
MONSANTA'S BRIDLE READY FOR
HIS APPEARANCE AT THE
BARCELONA OLYMPICS

Lindsay Brewerton has been a groom for Michael Whitaker for three years. Now 22-years old, she has been around horses since the age of five and had her own pony at home. Her father wasn't really horse minded but her mother supported her interest. She rode at Pony Club level. Before joining Michael's yard, she worked with dressage horses.

'I competed at local shows, jumped a little but I didn't have enough confidence to do the big stuff. Horses have always been a hobby rather than a career move. Anyway, I always preferred looking after them and watching them, than actually competing because you have to be so very good to really make it. I wanted to work for Michael because I wanted to learn. I have learned so much from working with show jumpers. I had never travelled around Europe. I never thought that I could do that.

'You have to learn all the aspects of it, but it is like a drug! Once you are into it, you can't get out! I think horses will always be part of my life. Probably not grooming. Not the mucking out, the getting up at seven in the morning and going to bed at one the next morning. I don't think that I could do that forever because I already feel like 40 now! But being at shows is fun too. I like being around people, making new friends. Plus if you are working for someone who is as good as Michael and you are winning, it is a good buzz. I don't think that I could work for any other rider on the circuit than Michael. But it is not glamorous at all.'

One of the pitfalls of caring for a particular horse is that you may find it hard to let go should the horse be sold. Cilla Leonard has been a groom for seven years, and found herself in just such circumstances. She now works for Italian rider Valerio Sozzi who was based at the Schockemöhle stable for a while. Having groomed for Peter Charles, she decided to leave England when the chance to go abroad arose. She joined Schockemöhle's yard and groomed for Otto Becker for three and a half years. Cilla used to look after the mare Pamina when Otto Becker rode her, but lost her when Pamina was sold to Valerio Sozzi. When Valerio came to train with Schockemöhle in Germany, Cilla was very happy to get Pamina back.

HORSES NORMALLY DON'T HAVE TO STAY IN A TENT BUT BECAUSE OF QUARANTINE REGULATIONS AT THE 1992 MASTERS IN SPRUCE MEADOWS, ALL THE EUROPEAN HORSES COMING FROM THE OLYMPICS WERE HOUSED IN TEMPORARY STABLING. CILLA LEONARD IS PICTURED WITH LEANDRA AND LUCKY LUKE. 'THIS WAS SORT OF A FAREWELL FOR ME AS I KNEW THAT OTTO WOULD BE LEAVING THE SCHOCKEMÖHLE STABLE SOON AFTER CALGARY. LUCKY LUKE IS NOT REALLY A BIG CHARACTER, BUT LEANDRA IS. I LIKE THEM BOTH A LOT. IT'S NICE TO SEE LEANDRA AT SHOWS BECAUSE SHE IS WELL LOOKED AFTER AND HAPPY BECAUSE SHE STILL HAS OTTO, HER FAVOURITE RIDER, THE ONLY ONE SHE WILL GO FOR'

(RIGHT) PENNY WILSON, GROOM TO JOHN WHITAKER, KEEPS MILTON COMPANY IN HIS STABLE AT THE 1992 BARCELONA OLYMPICS. ALTHOUGH THE BRITISH MASCOT WAS WATCHING OVER MILTON DURING THE OLYMPICS, HIS LUCK RAN OUT ON THE VERY LAST ROUND OF THE FINAL DAY

PEETER AITKEN, GROOM TO
AUSTRALIAN RIDER SUSAN BOND,
IS COMFORTING FRENCH KISS
BEFORE THE MAIN CLASS OF THE
DAY AT THE 1990 CSIO IN ROME

'You really get attached to horses — too attached especially when you work for Schockemöhle because they can get sold anytime. Pamina got sold to Valerio and here I am again! I got her back six months after

'Well, the first year I got Pamina, she was very successful. Then she had colic twice and no one else believed it because she gets really quiet. She doesn't go crazy with it. One time it was in

she got sold because Valerio came to Mühlen to train. I am not solely moving to Italy to be with Pamina but also because of better conditions, better pay and because I get along well with Valerio. This is very important. As a groom you have to be able to take orders from your boss but have a joke too! The riders have to have respect for you just as much as you have respect for them. They have to trust you.

Dortmund in 1991, I kept looking and looking at her. I was sure that there was something wrong with her, but although the vets had listened to her, they wouldn't believe that there was something wrong. I still stayed up all night with her and then she got really really bad. I got Otto out of bed and finally they believed me. I don't know what it is, but I have a feeling for her.

AMERICAN EAST COAST RIDERS ESCAPE THE WINTER MONTHS AND COMPETE ON THE FLORIDA CIRCUIT FROM THE BEGINNING OF FEBRUARY TO THE END OF MARCH. HERE, IN FEBRUARY 1988, AN AMERICAN GROOM AND HORSE ARE WAITING PATIENTLY UNDER A TREE, AWAY FROM THE HOT SUN OF TAMPA

Having a horse to love is only one side of the job, it's important to get on with the riders too. 'Otto used to not say much when he got out of the ring, but five minutes later when he got off the horse, or, after the class was finished, he would come back to the stable and discuss it more. It is also a matter of character. They are all different. Sometimes you also get the blame for something that happened in the ring. I remember one year at a national show, Otto showed me which studs he wanted me to put in. So I did. The horse slipped and Otto came out of the ring and started to scream. I just said look at the studs. He picked the foot up and said "No, no these are not the studs I wanted, I wanted the other ones." Sometimes you have got to have a thick skin. But this doesn't happen very often. The riders are under a lot of pressure and they come out of the ring and it's like

letting off steam. You happen to be there. . .

In one matter all the grooms were unanimous: 'Don't believe that it is glamourous'. Cilla continues:

AFTER THE FIRST JUMP OFF IN THE PUISSANCE AT AACHEN CSIO 1989 HORSES, GROOMS AND RIDERS, WHO ARE STILL IN THE COMPETITION, HAVE TO STAY IN A SPECIALLY FENCED OFF COLLECTING RING TO WAIT FOR THEIR TURN. HERE VANCOUVER, PUISSANCE SPECIALIST TO AUSTRIAN RIDER BORIS BOOR, AND HIS GROOM ARE CHECKING OUT THE OPPOSITION

'When I was young and I used to watch Wembley and Hickstead on TV and I used to see the groom throwing the blanket over Ryan's Son or Deister, I went Whoa, I'd love to do that when I'm older! Don't believe that it's just that. Now I am doing it, but I would probably tell people to work harder at school and try to do a *normal* job instead of this. There is

no real future in it really unless you have got some money at home and your family can help you to start up something at home. Working for foreign riders in foreign countries does give you the opportunity to learn another language though. Now that I am going to Italy, I have got to learn the language because no one there speaks anything else but Italian! This gives you more prospects for the future. You could put the languages into use and become a translator or something to do with languages.'

Being a groom is a vocation that only the dedicated can follow.

The spotlight is on the rider, and the prize-money always goes elsewhere, it does seem that all they have is a very special relationship with a very special horse.

YOU WILL NEVER SEE A GROOM AT THE RINGSIDE WITHOUT A TOWEL: IT IS USED TO WIPE THE RIDER'S BOOTS, SPURS, THE STIRRUP IRONS, THE BIT ETC. HERE, THE 1990 CSIO IN ROME, THE HORSE CARRIES THE TOWEL WHILE WAITING FOR THE RIDER TO ARRIVE

PRIZE-GIVING

I have mixed feelings about prize-giving ceremonies. On the one hand I think that prize-givings should be real moments of celebration. They are lovely for the winners, the supporters, the owners and the sponsors. The atmosphere with all the glitz and ceremony that surrounds it can be rather special. Depending on the event it can involve a lot of prestige.

Winning a major championship or an illustrious Grand Prix like that at Aachen can be such an emotional moment. My dislike comes into it when organisers don't seem to want to share the prize-giving ceremony. First of all they will place the photographers as far away as possible — just don't let the photographers inconvenience the proceedings! They will come up with a magic rope, place it in front of the photographers, and brief us that in no circumstances are we allowed beyond the rope. I do understand the thought behind the organisers' action. Then again it is our job to get an atmospheric moment imprinted on film, but I do wish that we got

'IN A MOMENT LIKE THIS YOU FEEL VERY GRATEFUL TO HAVE SUCH A TOP HORSE FOR THE OCCASION. EVERYBODY HAS TOP HORSES BUT TO HAVE THE RIGHT HORSE AT THE PRECISE MOMENT IS SPECIAL. I HAVE BEEN A PROFESSIONAL FOR 19 YEARS, SO I HAVE WAITED A LONG TIME FOR THIS INSTANT. I WAS NEVER IN A REAL HURRY BECAUSE I ALWAYS BELIEVED THAT I WOULD GET A HORSE LIKE RATINA Z ONE DAY SO THAT I COULD PROVE THAT I COULD DO IT. I ONLY RODE HER IN THE SECOND ROUND BECAUSE I HAD STAYED CLEAR IN THE FIRST AND I HAD A REAL CHANCE. ALL IN ALL, I FELT MORE EMOTIONAL WHEN WINNING THE TEAM GOLD BECAUSE WE ARE SUCH GOOD FRIENDS IN THE TEAM. WE TRUST EACH OTHER AND KNOW WHAT WE ARE CAPABLE OF ACHIEVING INDIVIDUALLY.
PIET RAYMAKERS (HOL) AND RATINA Z PICTURED AT THE INDIVIDUAL PRIZE-GIVING OF THE BARCELONA OLYMPICS, WHERE THEY WON A SILVER MEDAL

'AT THE VERY MOMENT THIS PICTURE WAS TAKEN, AND WHILE WE WERE ALREADY CELEBRATING BEFORE THE PROPER PRIZE-GIVING, I HADN'T YET REALISED THAT BY WINNING HERE IN AACHEN THE DUTCH TEAM HAD WRITTEN HISTORY. IT HAD BEEN ABOUT 40 YEARS SINCE A DUTCH TEAM WON THE NATIONS CUP IN AACHEN. IT WAS A FANTASTIC SUCCESS. NOT ONLY FOR ME BUT FOR THE WHOLE TEAM BECAUSE AACHEN IS RECOGNISED AS ONE OF THE BIGGEST SHOWS IN THE WORLD'
HANS HORN, DUTCH CHEF D'EQUIPE

'I REMEMBER THAT THERE WAS ONLY EGANO AND MILTON IN THE JUMP OFF. I WAS FIRST TO GO AND WENT FAST KNOWING THAT JOHN WAS GOING TO GO FOR IT. UNFORTUNATELY MILTON HURT HIMSELF AT THE SECOND FENCE AND JOHN PULLED HIM UP . . . SO I WON. IT IS ALWAYS A SPECIAL FEELING TO WIN — EVERYBODY DREAMS OF WINNING THE BEST GRAND PRIX OF THE YEAR SUCH AS MODENA OR CALGARY, THE ONES WHERE THE PRIZE-MONEY IS HIGH! EGANO IS A FUNNY HORSE, HE HAS A GREAT PERSONALITY, HE IS VERY NICE TO RIDE BUT HE CAN BE DIFFICULT IN THE STABLE'

JOS LANSINK (HOL) AND EGANO AT THE CSIO OF SAN MARINO 1991

treated with a little more respect.

It gets even more difficult if a member of the Royal Family is to present the Trophy. Security is even tighter. I understand that, because over the years royalty has been under a lot of pressure from the media. However, people do seem to forget that none of the equestrian photographers are remotely like the paparazzi photographers. We are not after a shot in which VIPs make fools of themselves. All we want is a picture of a happy looking Princess who will show joy and recognition for the winning partnership. Slim chance of that. The Princess Royal has made it a habit to walk up to the winner, shake hands as quickly as possible, deliberately turning her back on the photographers. Other personalities are delightful: I remember Prince Edward when he presented the prizes for the 1992 CSIO Nations Cup day in Hickstead. He had been most relaxed and charming, smiling at the cameras.

Sometimes I find it hard to believe that riders can be so reserved and introvert about their emotions. They just stand there and show no sign of happiness at all. Are they that used to winning? Does it just become routine and therefore of such little pleasure? or, are they really that shy? I know that it is difficult to show too much exuberance because the rider has to control his horse too, but I believe that compared to other sports such as tennis or football, rivals to prime-time television coverage, our personalities don't seem to shine so much.

One of the nicest shows when it comes to photographing prize-givings is Spruce Meadows. Ron

and Marg Southern, organisers/owners of the show, really know how to celebrate a win. Not only do they give the sponsors value for money by getting exposure to advertising etc, they also give the

photographers sufficient time to set up the shot. Ultimately the show jumpers benefit from sponsor support, and the sponsors benefit from media exposure.

Some riders really recognise that it is important to put something back into the sport. I remember when Joe Turi won the 1990 Hickstead Derby on Vital. The first three received a huge bouquet of flowers. Before his lap of honour Joe gave the flowers to a lady in the audience. I am sure that this gesture made her day. At shows like Gothenburg in Sweden the atmosphere is always electric. Fans come well-equipped with colourful banners plastered with their heroes' names. It was really nice to see riders like John Whitaker and Ludger Beerbaum acknowledge their fans at the 1993 Volvo World Cup Final. After the prize-giving they threw the chocolate Easter eggs they were given to their fans.

'I AM ALWAYS VERY HAPPY WHEN I WIN. IT IS THE CULMINATION OF A COMPETITION. THE WHOLE BUILD UP, SO MANY THINGS HAVE TO COME TOGETHER ON THE DAY, ALL THIS MAKES WINNING A GP RATHER SPECIAL FOR ME. I LIKE GIVING THE PUBLIC, THAT HAS BEEN WATCHING ENTHUSIASTICALLY, A SIGN OF RECOGNITION. THE PUBLIC HAS A RIGHT TO SEE HOW HAPPY ONE IS TO HAVE WON. I WOULD LIKE TO SEE THE RELATIONSHIP BETWEEN THE AUDIENCE AND THE RIDERS GROW EVEN CLOSER'

FRANKE SLOOTHAAK (GER) WINNING THE GRAND PRIX IN ROTTERDAM 1991 ON WALZERKÖNIG IN A THREE-WAY JUMP OFF

'IT WAS A VERY EXCITING MOMENT BECAUSE THE US TEAM CAME TO LANAKEN AS UNDERDOGS REALLY. WE WEREN'T EXPECTED TO WIN. THE US TEAM HADN'T DONE THAT WELL DURING THE YEAR. IT WAS SUCH FUN COMING TO LANAKEN AND GETTING IT DONE! THERE WAS A LOT OF ENTHUSIASM IN THE TEAM. WE ALL GOT ALONG SO WELL WHICH MADE IT HAPPEN'

LESLIE BURR LENEHAM OF THE US TEAM. THE NATIONS CUP TROPHY (SEPT 1991) WAS NOT WELL RECEIVED BY THE MEDIA AND LOST ITS SPONSOR, NEVERTHELESS THE FINAL WAS EXCITING. IT CAME TO A JUMP OFF BETWEEN GERMANY AND THE US

(RIGHT) 'TO WIN THE NATIONS CUP IN HICKSTEAD IN THIS MAGNIFICENT ARENA IS SIMPLY THE GREATEST FEELING! WE ALL KNOW THAT THE BRITISH TEAM IS ONE OF THE STRONGEST TEAMS AROUND AND THAT THEY ARE USUALLY HARD TO BEAT, ESPECIALLY ON THEIR HOME GROUND WHERE THEY SEEM UNLEASHED. WE HAVE A GREAT TEAM SPIRIT AND BIND TOGETHER SO WELL. THIS IS THE STRENGTH OF A TEAM. IT IS ALSO THE STRENGTH OF THE BRITISH TEAM, THEY ARE ALL FRIENDS'

MICHAEL ROBERT, TEAM MEMBER. THE FRENCH TEAM WON THE NATIONS CUP AT THE 1991 CSIO HICKSTEAD, BEATING THE BRITS INTO SECOND PLACE AFTER A JUMP OFF

'WINNING THE GRAND PRIX WAS A TURNING POINT IN NONIX'S CAREER. I
SURPRISED A LOT OF PEOPLE IN CHOOSING NONIX. NOT MANY BELIEVED IN
HIM, SOME MADE FUN OF ME ESPECIALLY AS THINGS HADN'T STARTED OFF
TOO WELL BETWEEN NONIX AND ME. MY WIN IN PARIS MADE SOME PEOPLE
FEEL UNEASY. FOR ME IT WAS MY OWN WAY OF PROVING THEM ALL
WRONG. ONE ALWAYS HAS TO HAVE HOPE AND BELIEVE. THIS WIN
TRIGGERED OFF A SERIES OF WINS FOR US, SUCH AS THE FRENCH
CHAMPIONSHIPS AND THE GRAND PRIX OF BORDEAUX. I BELIEVED IN NONIX
BECAUSE HE COVERS THE WHOLE SPECTRUM OF ASSETS A SHOW JUMPER
NEEDS. HE HAS COURAGE, A HUGE POTENTIAL AND NOTHING FRIGHTENS
HIM. SOMETIMES HE IS NOT EASY TO MANAGE. HIS FRAME IS VERY LIGHT
AND HE HAS A SENSITIVE BACK. I OWE NONIX A LOT'

MICHEL ROBERT (FR) WINNING THE GRAND PRIX AT THE 1991 PARIS MASTERS WITH NONIX

'THIS WAS PROBABLY THE MOST
EXCITING DAY OF MY CAREER —
WINNING THE GP IN AACHEN!
THIS IS WHERE STARMAN
BELONGS. HE IS BIG AND SCOPY.
HE LOVES THAT KIND OF
ATMOSPHERE, HE IS AT HIS BEST
IN THE TOUGHEST COMPETITION.
HE IS COURAGEOUS, A LITTLE
ARROGANT BUT TERRIBLY POLITE,
AND A DREAM TO RIDE'
ANNE KURSINSKI (USA) AND
STARMAN 1991

'I FELT A LOT RICHER! IT REALLY WAS GREAT ESPECIALLY AS IT CAME IMMEDIATELY AFTER THE EUROPEAN CHAMPIONSHIP WHERE I WAS JUST BEATEN INTO SECOND PLACE BY JOHN. I WAS VERY PLEASED FOR THE HORSE NOT JUST FOR ME. WHEN YOU ENTER THE RING ON MONSANTA, YOU KNOW THAT HE WILL ALWAYS GIVE HIS BEST. HE NEVER REALLY LETS YOU DOWN WHICH IS THE MOST IMPORTANT THING'

MICHAEL WHITAKER (GB) AND MONSANTA, SPRUCE MEADOWS, CALGARY 1989. THE PARTNERSHIP WON A RECORD £82,500 BY BEATING SWISS RIDER THOMAS FUCHS AND DOLLAR GIRL IN A GRUELLING JUMP OFF

(ABOVE) 'I HAVE ALWAYS HAD A LOT OF ADMIRATION, ESTEEM AND RESPECT FOR ERIC. I GOT TO APPRECIATE HIS QUALITIES AND HIS FRIENDSHIP BACK IN 1984 WHEN WE WERE ON THE SAME TEAM AT THE LOS ANGELES OLYMPICS. I FOUND IT RATHER SAD THAT BETWEEN THE END OF 1984 AND 1990, ERIC NEVER HAD THE TOP HORSES THAT WOULD HAVE ALLOWED HIM TO COMPETE AT THE TOP. HE WAS READY AND CAME BACK BEFORE STOCKHOLM, BUT HE STILL DOUBTED HIS AND QUITO'S ABILITIES. ERIC ALWAYS UNDERESTIMATES HIMSELF. OUT OF INTUITION, FRIENDSHIP, ESTEEM FOR ERIC AND OUT OF THE DESIRE TO HAVE HIM ON THE TEAM FOR THE WORLD CHAMPIONSHIPS, I CONVINCED HIM, HIS FATHER, AND PATRICK CARON THAT ERIC AND QUITO WERE MORE THAN READY. AFTER THE SHOW AT FRANCOVILLE ERIC FINALLY GAVE IN AND PLAYED THE GAME! I AM ABSOLUTELY DELIGHTED FOR HIM. HE DESERVES IT ALL'

PIERRE DURAND COMMENTS ON ERIC NAVET'S PERFORMANCE AT THE 1990 WORLD EQUESTRIAN GAMES

'CALGARY DOES SOMETHING TO ME, I DON'T QUITE KNOW WHAT, BUT IT BRINGS THE BEST OUT IN ME AND THE BEST OUT IN THE RIDERS. WE HAVE WON THE NATIONS CUP NINE TIMES OUT OF THE 15 YEARS THAT I HAVE BEEN TAKING A TEAM THERE. WHAT IS GREAT ABOUT CALGARY, IS THAT WE, THE BRITISH TEAM HAVE HELPED TO MAKE IT. WE WENT THERE 15 YEARS AGO FOR THE FIRST MASTERS AT CALGARY. BASED AT THE FOOT OF THE ROCKIES IN THE MONTH OF SEPTEMBER IT ISN'T ALWAYS BLESSED WITH THE BEST WEATHER— WE HAVE HAD SOME TERRIBLE YEARS WITH RAIN, WIND, EVEN SNOWSTORMS, BUT WE STUCK IN THERE AND KEPT COMING BACK. WE SAW THE CROWDS RISE FROM A TOTAL OF 2,500 OVER THE FIVE DAYS TO WELL OVER 130,000 PEOPLE AND I FEEL THAT THE BRITISH TEAM IS PART OF WHAT MADE THAT SHOW. THE FIRST YEAR HARVEY SMITH WAS SINGING SOLO AND CONDUCTED A GREAT PARTY ONE EVENING. THE CAMARADERIE

BETWEEN ALL THE TEAMS AND THE SOUTHERN FAMILY WHO RUN THE SHOW IS UNIQUE.
BACK IN 1977 SPRUCE MEADOWS LOOKED LIKE A CATTLE LOCK AND I ALWAYS SAY THAT IT HAS BEEN SOME GREAT CATTLE LOCK FOR THE BRITS, WE HAVE WON THOUSANDS AND THOUSANDS OF DOLLARS THERE! WE SEEM TO ALWAYS COME OUT ON TOP. IT IS JUST A MAGICAL SHOW AS FAR AS WE ARE CONCERNED'
RONNIE MASSARELLA COMMENTS ON THE 1992 SPRUCE MEADOWS MASTERS THE BRITISH TEAM WON THE BANK OF MONTREAL NATIONS CUP FOR A RECORD FOURTH TIME IN A ROW

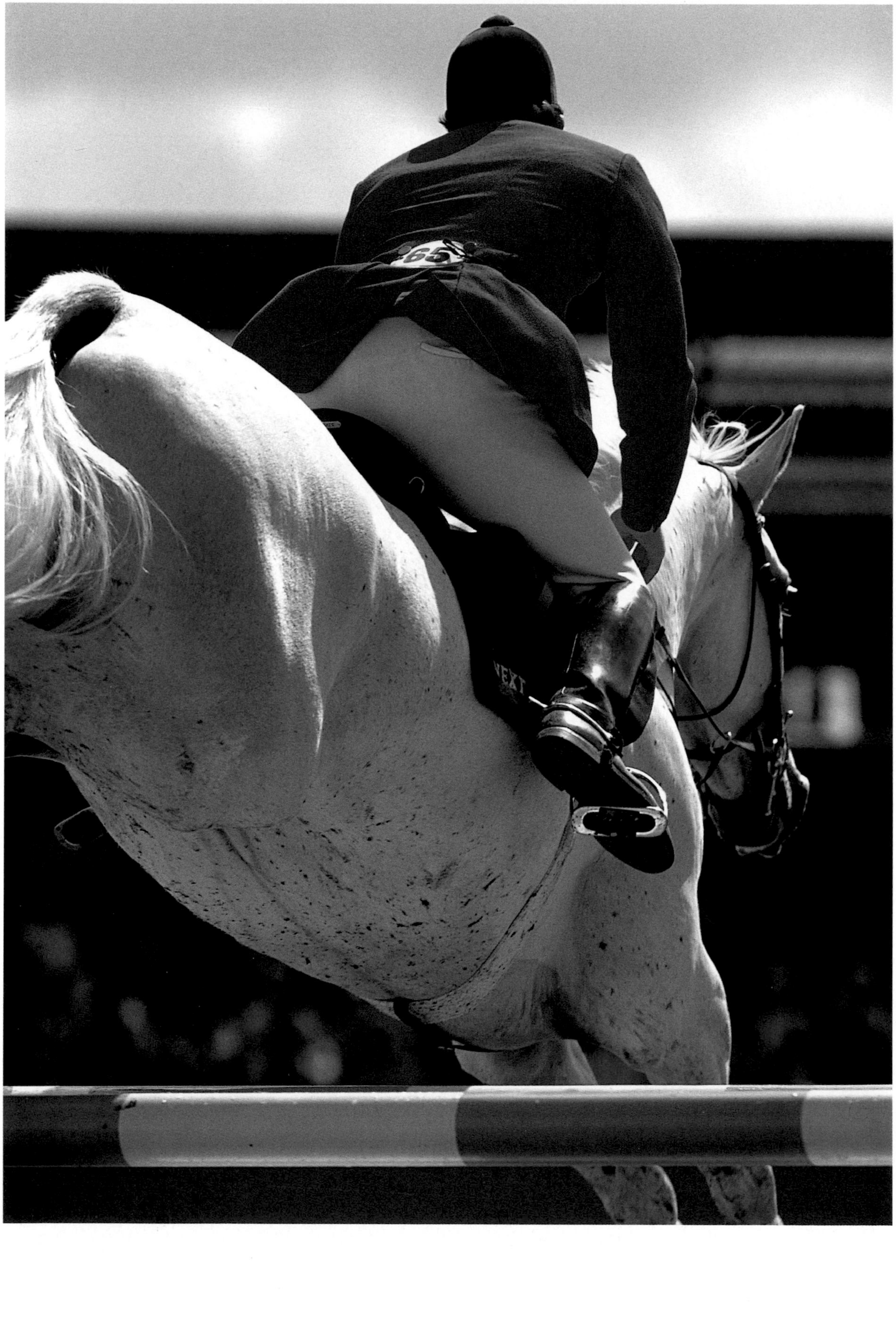

LASTING IMPRESSIONS

Wherever we go, whichever activity we undertake, we usually come away from it with a lasting impression. If we go on holiday, to the theatre, the cinema, a concert, a restaurant, or simply when we meet people, a particular aspect of our experience goes with us. I believe that it is a strong characteristic of human nature that we want things to last. It is nice to have fond memories of the enjoyable things in life.

Going to a horse show is no different. Whenever I attend an international horse show, I come away from it with at least one memorable experience that I will treasure, and that stays with me for a long time. It is not that I go to a horse show with expectations of all moments being eventful, on the contrary, it is always overwhelming when it actually does happen. Being a photographer, it is somewhat in the nature of my job to turn split seconds into something everlasting. Yes, photography helps! Photographs can catch moments that are out of the ordinary and I do try to set out to achieve it.

Often when in the ring I see images that I would dearly like to capture on film, but either they go by so fast or I am not in the right spot for them. I remember the first year I was photographing the Grand Prix in Rotterdam, we were allowed in the arena. I chose a spot bang next to the treble

combination so that I could catch the riders as they were jumping into it. I was quite close to the middle element, an oxer, with a head on view of the first fence. Many riders went by and I got nice, riders-looking-up type of pictures. After a while it was John Whitaker's turn, riding Hopscotch: he jumped in, I took the picture, he landed, took a stride, and in mid-air while jumping the second element of the treble, he casually changed his whip from his left hand over the horse's neck to his right hand, and landed. Giving Hopscotch a slight reminder with the whip on the non-jumping stride, he jumped out of the combination in great style. I simply stood there in amazement! I was taken back by John's incredible feeling. Not only was he able to execute this change over in the most agile and yet, to the horse, inconspicuous manner, but he also felt so early on that Hopscotch was swaying to the right and succeeded in avoiding a run out. Witnessing this at such close range, really left me with a lasting impression. In addition it also taught me to follow a rider through the lens as long as possible. I would have simply loved to catch that change over on a sequence of shots.

Lasting impressions also motivate you to fight on. They are moments of joy we can draw from when things are not running too smoothly. Remembering

BACK VIEW OF JOHN AND MILTON TAKEN AT A HICKSTEAD MEETING IN 1988 feelings of success helps people through times when everything seems to go wrong. Moments of ups and downs happen quite frequently in the world of show jumping. In fact, I always admire riders who appear to overcome dry periods so well. I often wonder where they find their strength to fight back. Riders have told me that it's not only by means of projected visions and positive thoughts, it is also by making use of their unforgettable moments of glory.

Wouldn't it be nice if all lasting impressions were positive ones? Unfortunately this is not always the case. Riders as well as horses remember bad moments just as much as they do the good ones. Horses too have a sense for remembering things that they have done in the past. They recognise places they have been, and things that might not have gone too well.

On one occasion John Whitaker had loaned Hopscotch to Nick Skelton to ride in the 1990 Hickstead Derby. Nick rode Hopscotch very well and

was clear up to the top of the Bank when Hopscotch took Nick by surprise, stopping at the little rail on top of the Bank. The year before when ridden by John, Hopscotch had done the same thing. At the 1991 Derby Hopscotch, back to his usual rider John, went up the bank again. This time John put a little more pressure on the horse before getting to the rail. Hopscotch jumped but sadly, as you can see in the Mishaps Chapter, he had a slight difficulty coming down the bank. The following year, John took Hopscotch to the outdoor Millstreet Derby. When reaching the top of the bank, Hopscotch didn't want to come down it. After two attempts of trying to convince Hopscotch, John decided to retire him. I believe that the horse probably remembered the Hickstead incident. Some horses are more sensitive to things like that than others. Some seem to be able to overcome bad moments.

Sometimes negative lasting impressions provoke a feeling of superstition amongst riders. Veronique

DAVID BROOME AND PETER
CHARLES WALKING THE COURSE
AT THE 1990 CSIO ROME. RIDERS
ARE ALWAYS COMPARING NOTES
BEFORE A BIG CLASS.

Whitaker doesn't want to take her mare Flarepath back to a Hickstead meeting. During the 1992 Queen Elizabeth II Cup staged at the All England Show Ground, Flarepath injured her tendon which resulted in the mare needing a lay-off period of well over six months.

The lasting impressions I have selected for this chapter are however on a much happier note. They range from portraits of the riders to smiles, hugs, still life images and moments of concentration.

**GEM TWIST STANDS WITH FRANK
CHABOT THE US** *CHEF D'EQUIPE*
**AND TRAINER OF GREG BEST, AT
THE 1990 WORLD EQUESTRIAN
GAMES**

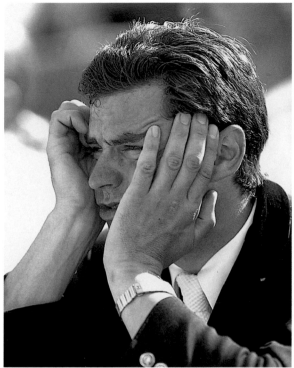

(LEFT) OTTO BECKER (GER) IN THE COMPETITORS ENCLOSURE DURING THE 1991 MASTERS IN SPRUCE MEADOWS. OTTO'S GREATEST WORRY WAS WHETHER HE COULD DEFEND THE DU MAURIER GRAND PRIX TITLE HE HAD WON THERE THE PREVIOUS YEAR

(LEFT) THOMAS FRÜHMANN (AUSTRIA) AFTER THE FIRST LEG OF THE 1990 WORLD EQUESTRIAN GAMES. THOMAS, REPRESENTING AUSTRIA AS AN INDIVIDUAL, FACED THE TOUGH FACT THAT HIS MOUNT CORNADO WASN'T REALLY UP TO THE STRAIN OF THE CHAMPIONSHIPS

MARK TODD (NZ), 1992 RIHS AT HICKSTEAD

JOHN AND MICHAEL WHITAKER (GB) IN LA BAULE 1991 AFTER THE BRITISH TEAM HAD WON THE TEAM SILVER MEDAL AT THE EUROPEAN CHAMPIONSHIPS. MEMBERS OF THE BRITISH PRESS IMPROVISED A SMALL PRESS CONFERENCE ON THE STANDS RIGHT AFTER THE PRIZE-GIVING. 'IT LOOKS AS IF JOHN MUST HAVE JUST SAID SOMETHING REALLY SILLY! JOHN AND I GET ALONG VERY WELL. I DON'T SEE MUCH OF HIM REALLY, ONLY AT SHOWS, WHICH IS EVERY WEEKEND! I NEVER WORRY ABOUT JOHN'S PERFORMANCE IN A NATIONS CUP. HE IS VERY RELIABLE. I THINK HE WORRIES ABOUT ME THOUGH'

THE CARABINIERI REPRESENT THE ITALIAN MOUNTED POLICE. THEY USUALLY ENTERTAIN AT BIG SHOWS IN ITALY SUCH AS DURING THE CSIOS OF ROME AND MODENA. HERE THEY ARE ON DUTY AT THE 1992 CSIO OF SAN MARINO (BELOW) THE 1990 CSIO ROME

THIS SHOT WAS TAKEN IN A
SPEED CLASS DURING THE 1990
CSIO AACHEN. IT WAS TAKEN AT
A 60TH OF A SECOND AND GIVES
A SENSE OF MOVEMENT

AT THE 1990 STOCKHOLM WORLD EQUESTRIAN GAMES
LINDA BRIGGS AND ROS REED CELEBRATE TEN YEARS OF
GOING TO ALL THE MAJOR CHAMPIONSHIPS. THEY ARE
FOUNDER MEMBERS OF THE SHOW JUMPING SUPPORTERS'
CLUB GB WHICH BEGAN IN DECEMBER 1992.
'WE TRY TO GO TO AT LEAST TWO OR THREE
INTERNATIONAL SHOWS A YEAR. ONE OF THE MOST
ENJOYABLE THINGS ABOUT TRAVELLING TO SHOWS
ABROAD IS MEETING PEOPLE FROM OTHER COUNTRIES
WITH THE SAME INTEREST. IT IS NICE TO COMPARE
EXPERIENCES. IT IS ALSO A GOOD OPPORTUNITY TO SEE
THE TOP FOREIGN RIDERS THAT WE DON'T SEE IN THE
UK VERY MUCH AT ALL. BUT ABOVE ALL, WE LIKE TO SEE
THE BRITISH DO WELL'

(BELOW) THE SWEDISH CROWD
IS WELL KNOWN FOR ITS
COLOURFUL SUPPORTERS. HERE
AT THE 1993 VOLVO WORLD CUP
FINAL GOTHENBURG, LUDGER
BEERBAUM'S FANS ARE CHEERING
THE WINNER

(ABOVE) JOHN WHITAKER,
WINNER OF THE FINAL IN
GOTHENBURG 1991, IS ALWAYS
A WELCOME VISITOR TO THE
SCANDINAVIUM AND HAS HIS
SHARE OF FAITHFUL
SUPPORTERS TOO

1993 VOLVO WORLD CUP FINAL
IN GOTHENBURG. LUDGER
BEERBAUM IS HOLDING A
PRESENT GIVEN BY AN ADMIRER

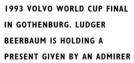

PAUL DARRAGH (IRL) WALKING
THE GRAND PRIX COURSE AT THE
1992 CSIO HICKSTEAD

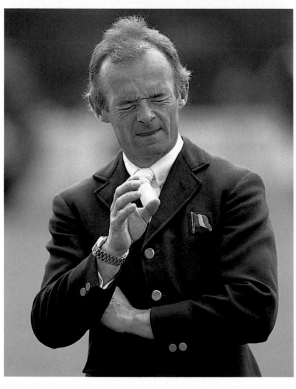

THE QUEEN ELIZABETH II CUP AT THE RIHS 1992 WAS HELD FOR THE FIRST TIME AT HICKSTEAD. THIS BRITISH DUO OF TRACY PRIEST AND HARDEN DILWYN HAD JUST COMPLETED THEIR FIRST ROUND. I AM SURE THAT THE PICTURE GIVES THEIR RESULT AWAY! AFTER THE JUMP OFF THEY LINED UP IN FOURTH PLACE.

'DILLY SEEMS TO ALWAYS FIND ANOTHER FOOT OF SCOPE WHEN GOING ROUND HICKSTEAD. I WOULD SAY HE IS A ONE OFF, A HORSE THAT EVERYBODY DREAMS OF HAVING IN A LIFE TIME'

KATIE MONAHAN PRUDENT

NELSON PESSOA

PAUL DARRAGH

MICHEL ROBERT

ROGER-YVES BOST

HANS HORN

MARIE EDGAR

PATRICK CARON

MICHAEL WHITAKER

WILLI MELLIGER

IAN D MILLAR

TINA CASSAN

LUIS ALVAREZ

THOMAS FRÜHMANN

OTTO BECKER

MICHAEL MATZ

COLLEEN BROOK

ROBERT SMITH

ERIC NAVET

J C VANGEENBERGHE

PAUL WEIER

TRACY PRIEST

PIERRE DURRAND

FRANKE SLOOTHAAK

OLAF PETERSEN

ERIC WAUTERS

TIM GRUBB

JENNY ZOER

LUDGER BEERBAUM

HUGO SIMON